Holiday Celebration Dinner

Salmon Loaf Appetizer

Layered Salad

Jamaican Jerk Pork Loin

Vicki's Potatoes

Fresh, Crisp and Sweet Green Beans

Fruit Cocktail Cake

Apricot Nectar Cake

Salmon Loaf Appetizer

1 (1-pound) can salmon
1 (8-ounce) package cream cheese, softened
1 tablespoon lemon juice
2 teaspoons grated onion
¼ teaspoon salt
1 teaspoon prepared horseradish
¼ teaspoon liquid smoke
½ cup chopped pecans
3 tablespoons snipped fresh parsley

Drain and flake salmon removing any skin and bones. Add cream cheese, lemon juice, onion, salt, horseradish and liquid smoke. Mix thoroughly and shape into a loaf. Cover with plastic wrap and chill several hours. Combine pecans and parsley. Remove plastic wrap from loaf and roll in nut mixture. Cover and chill well. Serve with crackers. Yield: 12 servings.

Layered Salad

1 pound fresh spinach, torn into bite-size pieces
1 medium head lettuce, torn into bite-size pieces
6 hard-boiled eggs, sliced
1 pound bacon, cooked and crumbled
1 (8-ounce) can sliced water chestnuts, drained
1 (10-ounce) package frozen English peas, thawed
1 cup mayonnaise (or salad dressing)
½ cup sour cream
1 (1-ounce) package dry Hidden Valley Ranch dressing mix
Chopped fresh parsley for garnish, optional

In a large salad bowl, layer first 6 ingredients in order listed. In a separate bowl, add mayonnaise, sour cream and dressing mix; combine well. Spread over top of vegetables, sealing to edge of bowl. Garnish with chopped parsley, if desired. Cover tightly and refrigerate several hours or overnight. Toss gently before serving. Yield: 12 to 15 servings.

Note: I layer this salad in a punch bowl. It is beautiful, and the extra size of the bowl makes it easy to toss. Do this at the table.

Jamaican Jerk Pork Loin

2 (1½- to 2-pound) pork tenderloins (or 1 (2- to 3-pound) pork loin)
2 tablespoons chopped fresh cilantro
¼ teaspoon ground ginger
¼ cup rum
2 tablespoons fresh lime juice
2 tablespoons olive oil
2 tablespoons light brown sugar
2 tablespoons soy sauce
½ teaspoon nutmeg
¼ teaspoon cayenne
¼ teaspoon ground allspice
¼ teaspoon ground cinnamon
¼ teaspoon salt

Place pork in a flat baking dish. For marinade, combine remaining ingredients. Reserve a third of the marinade, and pour remaining marinade over pork. Cover and let sit 30 minutes to 1 hour at room temperature. Grill pork until internal temperature is 160°. Slice pork on the diagonal and place on a serving platter. Spoon reserved marinade over the pork and serve. Yield: 6 servings.

Vicki's Potatoes

6 medium potatoes, cooked, cooled and shredded
¼ cup butter, melted
1 (10.75-ounce) can cream of chicken soup
½ pint sour cream
1 cup grated Cheddar cheese
½ onion, chopped
½ teaspoon salt

Mix all ingredients together. Place in a casserole dish and bake at 300° for 1½ hours. Yield: 12 servings.

Fresh, Crisp and Sweet Green Beans

½ to 1 pound fresh green beans, cut into thirds
¼ to ½ cup golden raisins
Olive oil
¼ to ½ cup chopped smoked almonds
¼ to ½ cup chopped pimento-stuffed green olives

Boil green beans in salted water until crisp-tender. Add raisins about 30 seconds before beans are ready. Pour off water and add olive oil just to cover bottom of pan. Add chopped almonds and olives. Heat and serve. Yield: 4 to 6 servings.

Note: I use a food processor to chop the almonds and olives.

Fruit Cocktail Cake

2¼ cups flour
1½ cups sugar
1½ teaspoons baking soda
½ teaspoon salt

1 (15.25-ounce) can fruit cocktail
2 eggs
½ cup brown sugar
½ cup grated coconut

Sift flour, sugar, baking soda and salt. Beat in juice from fruit cocktail along with the eggs. Fold in fruit cocktail. Pour batter into greased and floured 9x13-inch cake pan and top with brown sugar and coconut. Bake at 325° for 35 to 45 minutes. Yield: 12 squares.

FROSTING:

1 stick butter
¾ cup sugar
½ cup evaporated milk

1 teaspoon vanilla extract
½ cup grated coconut

Mix butter, sugar and evaporated milk in a saucepan. Boil 2 minutes, stirring constantly. Stir in vanilla and coconut. Pour over warm cake.

Apricot Nectar Cake

1 package plain yellow cake mix
1 (3-ounce) package lemon Jell-O
¾ cup canned apricot nectar
¾ cup vegetable oil
1 teaspoon grated lemon zest
4 large eggs

Heat oven to 325°. Spray a 12-cup Bundt pan with vegetable oil and dust with flour. Place cake mix, gelatin, apricot nectar, oil, lemon zest and eggs in a mixing bowl; blend on low 1 minute. Stop and scrape down the sides with a rubber spatula. Increase mixer speed to medium and mix 2 to 3 minutes. Batter will be thick and smooth. Pour into prepared Bundt pan and bake about 40 minutes. Remove cake from oven when done and cool 10 minutes. While cake is cooling, prepare Glaze.

GLAZE:

¾ cup powdered sugar
4 tablespoons apricot nectar, or more if needed
2 tablespoons fresh lemon juice

Combine all Glaze ingredients in a small saucepan and cook over medium to low heat 3 to 4 minutes until the sugar dissolves.

Invert cake onto serving platter and prick holes in the top with a toothpick. Spoon Glaze over cake, allowing the Glaze to seep into the holes. Yield: 12 servings.

Holiday Dinner Party

Trio's Spinach Dip

Easy Romaine Green Salad
with Caesar Dressing

Sweet Bourbon Salmon Fillet

Broccoli-Rice Casserole

Sautéed Julienne Carrots

Roasted Asparagus

Piña Colada Cheesecake

Fuzzy Navel Cake

Trio's Spinach Dip

1 (10-ounce) package frozen chopped spinach, thawed and squeezed dry
⅔ cup milk or half-and-half
2 cups shredded Monterey Jack cheese
1 (8-ounce) package cream cheese, softened
1 (14.5-ounce) can Rotel tomatoes with green chiles, drained
1 onion, shredded
Salt and pepper to taste
Garlic powder and chili powder to taste

Mix all ingredients in an oven-proof dish. Bake at 400° for 30 to 40 minutes. Serve with chips, crackers and/or pita chips. Yield: 12 servings.

Easy Romaine Green Salad with Caesar Dressing

1 (1.2-ounce) package dry Caesar salad dressing mix, plus ingredients to prepare
1 pound fresh romaine lettuce leaves, torn
Croutons, optional

Prepare salad dressing according to package directions and chill. Place torn romaine in a large salad bowl. Toss greens with prepared dressing just before serving. Add croutons. Yield: 6 to 8 servings.

Sweet Bourbon Salmon Fillet

The marinade can be used on any type of fish.

¼ cup pineapple juice
2 tablespoons soy sauce
2 tablespoons brown sugar
1 teaspoon bourbon (or cognac)
¼ teaspoon black pepper

Dash garlic powder
½ cup vegetable oil
2 teaspoons chopped chives
1 salmon fillet

For marinade, combine all ingredients except the salmon. Place salmon in a flat baking dish and pour marinade over salmon. Cover and chill at least 1 hour. Grill or broil salmon fillets. Yield: approximately 1 cup marinade.

Broccoli-Rice Casserole

1 (10-ounce) package frozen chopped broccoli
½ cup chopped onion
1 stick butter, divided
1 (8-ounce) jar Cheez Whiz

1 (10.75-ounce) can cream of mushroom soup
Tabasco to taste
1½ cups cooked rice
Crushed Ritz crackers

Cook broccoli according to package directions; drain well. Sauté onion in half stick butter. Stir in Cheez Whiz, soup, Tabasco and rice. Pour into a buttered casserole dish. Top with crushed Ritz crackers and dot with remaining butter. Bake at 375° for 30 minutes. Yield: 8 to 12 servings.

Sautéed Julienne Carrots

2 pounds julienned or shoestring carrots
1 tablespoon vegetable oil
½ teaspoon nutmeg
½ teaspoon salt
Dash pepper
2 tablespoons water
¼ cup butter, melted

Place carrots in electric skillet and toss with oil, nutmeg, salt, pepper and water. Cook on medium heat, covered, stirring occasionally, 10 to 15 minutes or until tender. Remove from heat and toss with melted butter. Yield: 6 servings.

Roasted Asparagus

1 bunch fresh asparagus
1 tablespoon Dijon mustard
3 tablespoons balsamic vinegar
¼ cup extra virgin olive oil
¼ cup grated Parmesan cheese

Preheat oven to 450°. Snap off the tough ends of asparagus and discard. Whisk mustard and vinegar and slowly add olive oil as you continue whisking. Toss asparagus with the vinaigrette. Sprinkle with Parmesan cheese and spread evenly on a baking sheet. Roast 10 minutes. Yield: 2 to 4 servings.

Piña Colada Cheesecake

1½ cups vanilla wafer (or graham cracker) crumbs
½ cup flaked coconut, optional
3 tablespoons butter, melted
3 (8-ounce) packages cream cheese, softened
3 eggs
1 cup sugar
1 (8-ounce) can crushed pineapple, drained
1 cup sour cream
3 tablespoons dark rum
2 teaspoons coconut extract

Preheat oven to 350°. In medium bowl, combine cookie crumbs, coconut and melted butter. Press into bottom of a 9-inch springform pan. Bake 10 minutes. Cool.

In large mixing bowl, beat cream cheese, eggs and sugar. Stir in drained pineapple, sour cream, rum and coconut extract. Pour mixture into prepared crust. Bake 50 to 55 minutes or until set. Cool to room temperature; refrigerate until chilled. Spread Pineapple Topping over cheesecake just before serving. Yield: 16 servings.

PINEAPPLE TOPPING:

1 (20-ounce) can crushed pineapple, undrained
½ cup sugar
1 tablespoon dark rum
1 tablespoon cornstarch

Combine all topping ingredients in a large saucepan. Cook, stirring constantly, until thickened and clear. Cool before spreading over cake.

Fuzzy Navel Cake

1 package plain yellow cake mix
1 (5.1-ounce) package vanilla instant pudding mix
¾ cup peach schnapps
½ cup vegetable oil
½ cup fresh orange juice
4 large eggs
½ teaspoon orange extract

Heat oven to 350°. Lightly spray a 12-cup Bundt pan with vegetable spray and dust with flour. Place dry cake mix, pudding mix, schnapps, oil, orange juice, eggs and orange extract in a large mixing bowl and blend at low speed 1 minute. Scrape the sides down and mix on medium speed 2 minutes. The batter will be thick and smooth. Pour batter into prepared pan and bake 45 to 50 minutes. Remove from oven when done and cool 20 minutes. Prepare Glaze while cake cools.

GLAZE:

1 cup powdered sugar
2 tablespoons peach schnapps
4 tablespoons fresh orange juice

Place all Glaze ingredients in a small bowl and stir until blended. Invert cake onto serving plate and poke holes in top of cake using a toothpick. Spoon Glaze over cake, allowing it to seep into cake. Yield: 12 servings.

Christmas Shopping Brunch

Mimosas

Sausage Egg Bake

Green Chile Egg Squares

Garlic-Cheese Grits

Hash Brown Potato Casserole

Kay's Sausage Balls

Curried Fruit

Raspberry Cream Cheese
Coffee Cake

Serve With:
*Bacon and Ham
Biscuits with Assorted
Jams and Jellies
Coffee*

What a wonderful way to send your family and friends off for an afternoon of Christmas shopping! A relaxed gathering with good food prepares all for the crowds awaiting them at the malls. Everything can be prepared the day before, and then cooked right before your guests arrive. This way you're not tired and can join in on the shopping. Even your bacon and ham can be cooked, wrapped in foil, and then placed in the oven to warm while other dishes are cooking.

Mimosas

1 (12-ounce) can frozen concentrated orange juice, defrosted
6 cups champagne, chilled
Mint sprigs, optional

Prepare orange juice in a punch bowl according to directions on can. Add champagne, and serve. Garnish with mint sprigs.

Sausage Egg Bake

8 slices white bread, crusts trimmed
Butter, softened
1 pound ground pork sausage
2 cups shredded Cheddar cheese

6 large eggs, beaten
2 cups half-and-half
½ teaspoon salt
⅛ teaspoon black pepper

Butter each slice of bread on 1 side. Place bread, butter side up, in a 9x13-inch pan treated with cooking spray. Brown sausage in a skillet until cooked and crumbled. Drain sausage and place over bread slices. Sprinkle with cheese. Combine eggs, half-and-half, salt and pepper; pour over top. Cover and chill at least 8 hours. Remove from refrigerator and let sit 30 minutes. Bake, uncovered, in a 350° oven 45 minutes or until golden brown. Yield: 8 servings.

Green Chile Egg Squares

10 small eggs, beaten
1 (24-ounce) carton cottage cheese
2 cans chopped green chiles sprinkled with garlic salt
3 cups shredded Monterey Jack cheese

Mix all ingredients together and bake in a greased 9x13-inch baking dish at 350° for 30 minutes. Slice into small squares and serve hot or cold. Yield: 24 squares.

Note: I mix this up the day before and chill in a plastic container until ready to bake.

Garlic-Cheese Grits

1 cup quick-cooking grits	½ stick butter
4 cups water	¼ cup milk
1 (10-ounce) roll garlic cheese	Paprika to taste
2 eggs, beaten	

Preheat oven to 375°. Cook grits with water according to package directions. In a small bowl, combine beaten eggs, butter and milk. Stir slowly into grits mixing quickly to avoid cooking eggs. Pour into greased baking dish 15 to 30 minutes. Yield: 8 to 10 servings.

Hash Brown Potato Casserole

This can be made the day before and refrigerated.
Leftovers are great warmed in the microwave.

2 pounds frozen Southern Style Hash Browns, defrosted	2 cups sour cream
1 stick butter, melted	1 teaspoon salt
1 (10.75-ounce) can cream of chicken soup	½ teaspoon black pepper
	½ cup chopped, onion
	2 cups grated Cheddar cheese

Mix all ingredients well. Place in a buttered 9x13-inch baking dish.

TOPPING:

2 cups crushed corn flakes	½ stick butter, melted

Combine crushed corn flakes with melted butter. Sprinkle evenly over casserole. Bake at 350° for 40 to 45 minutes or until bubbly. Yield: 12 servings.

Note: May substitute ½ cup shredded cheese for the Topping.

Kay's Sausage Balls

1 pound sausage
1 (8-ounce) can water chestnuts, drained and chopped
Louisiana hot sauce to taste
2 (8-count) cans Texas-size biscuits (or Grands biscuits)

Mix sausage, water chestnuts and hot sauce. Form into ¾-inch balls. Broil and cool. Cut each canned biscuits into thirds. Wrap each ball with a third of a biscuit; seal. Bake until brown at the temperature recommended for the canned biscuits. Yield: 48 balls.

Curried Fruit

1 (15-ounce) can pineapple tidbits, drained, reserve ¾ cup juice
1 (15.25-ounce) can fruit cocktail, drained
1 (8-ounce) jar maraschino cherries, drained
1 (15-ounce) can apricots, drained

1 (15-ounce) can peach halves, drained
1 (15-ounce) can pear halves, drained
¼ cup brown sugar
¼ cup sugar
2 tablespoons cornstarch
1 teaspoon curry powder
¼ cup melted butter

Combine drained fruits in a 9x13-inch baking dish. Mix sugars, cornstarch, curry powder and reserved pineapple juice in a saucepan. Heat until it thickens slightly. Add melted butter; pour over fruits. Bake, covered, 30 minutes at 350°. Uncover and bake another 10 minutes. Yield: 12 servings.

Note: This is better if mixed up the day before cooking and refrigerated overnight. This is great as a leftover, and microwaves well.

Raspberry Cream Cheese Coffee Cake

2¼ cups all-purpose flour
1 cup sugar, divided
¾ cup cold butter
½ teaspoon baking powder
½ teaspoon baking soda
¼ teaspoon salt
¾ cup sour cream
1 teaspoon almond extract
2 eggs, divided
1 (8-ounce) package cream cheese, softened
½ cup raspberry preserves
½ cup sliced almonds

Heat oven to 350°. Grease and flour bottom and sides of a 9-inch or 10-inch springform pan. In large bowl, combine flour and ¾ cup sugar. Using pastry blender or fork, cut in butter until mixture resembles coarse crumbs. Reserve 1 cup of crumb mixture. To remaining crumb mixture, add baking powder, baking soda, salt, sour cream, almond extract and 1 egg; blend well. Spread batter over bottom and 2 inches up sides of prepared pan. (Batter should be about ¼-inch thick on sides.)

In small bowl, combine cream cheese, remaining ¼ cup sugar and remaining egg; blend well. Pour into batter-lined pan. Carefully spoon preserves evenly over cream cheese mixture. In small bowl, combine reserved crumb mixture and sliced almonds. Sprinkle over preserves.

Bake at 350° for 45 to 55 minutes or until cream cheese filling is set and crust is deep golden brown. Cool 15 minutes. Remove sides of pan. Serve warm or cool, cut into wedges. Store in refrigerator. Yield: 16 servings.

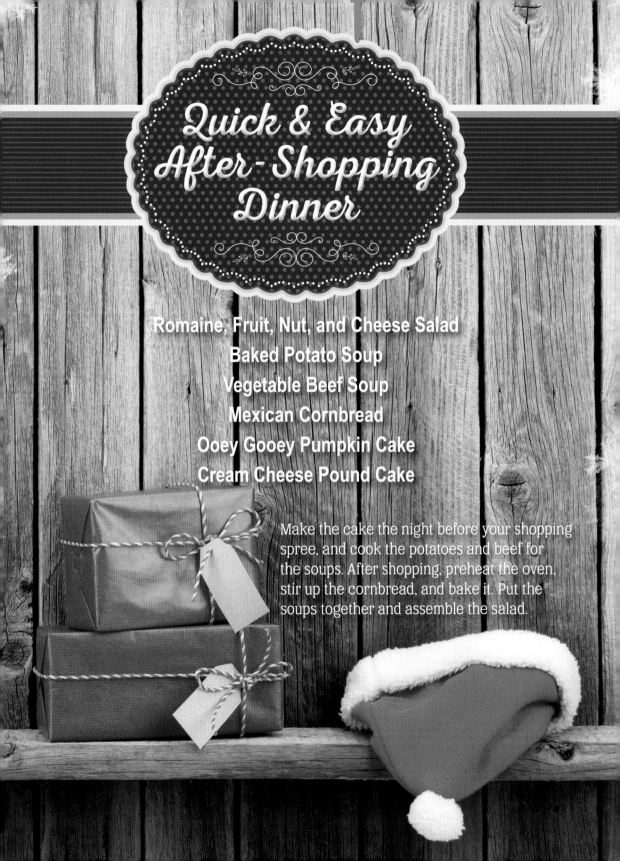

Quick & Easy After-Shopping Dinner

Romaine, Fruit, Nut, and Cheese Salad
Baked Potato Soup
Vegetable Beef Soup
Mexican Cornbread
Ooey Gooey Pumpkin Cake
Cream Cheese Pound Cake

Make the cake the night before your shopping spree, and cook the potatoes and beef for the soups. After shopping, preheat the oven, stir up the cornbread, and bake it. Put the soups together and assemble the salad.

Romaine, Fruit, Nut and Cheese Salad

1 (8- to 10-ounce) package chopped
  romaine lettuce
½ cup dried cranberries

¼ cup sliced almonds
¼ cup crumbled blue cheese
Blue cheese salad dressing

This salad can have many variations if you change the fruit, nuts, cheese and dressings. In the summer you can use fresh fruit such as strawberries, blueberries, melons, raspberries and cherries, just to name a few. You can also use fresh fruit in the fall and winter such as apples, pears, grapefruit and oranges. Pecans, almonds, peanuts, walnuts, pine nuts, macadamia nuts and others are always available to choose from. Cheese choices are many, as are salad dressings, so just choose the ones you like. There is no end to the many different tastes you can have by mixing the ingredients. Yield: 6 to 8 servings.

Baked Potato Soup

5 to 6 medium-size potatoes, peeled and
  cooked in water
1 (10.75-ounce) can cream of mushroom
  or chicken soup
1 (8-ounce) carton sour cream
1 (8-ounce) carton French onion dip

1 cup shredded Cheddar cheese
5 slices crisp bacon, crumbled
Milk (or chicken broth) to taste
Chopped chives, bacon crumbles,
  shredded cheese for garnish, optional

Slightly mash cooked potatoes and add soup, sour cream, dip, shredded cheese and crumbled bacon. Add milk to get the consistency you want. Garnish as desired. Yield: 8 to 12 servings, depending on consistency chosen.

Vegetable Beef Soup

2 pounds chuck roast or English roast, cut in cubes
1 medium onion, chopped
1 teaspoon minced garlic
2 tablespoons oil
1½ cups water
1 (1-pound) can tomatoes, undrained

2 (15-ounce) cans Veg-All, undrained
1 tablespoon salt
½ teaspoon marjoram
½ teaspoon thyme
1 bay leaf
1 cup raw elbow macaroni
Shredded cheese for garnish

Brown beef, onion and garlic in oil in a pressure cooker. Drain fat and add water. Cook in pressure cooker on high 20 minutes. While meat is cooking, pour remaining ingredients in a Dutch oven. Add cooked beef and juices to the Dutch oven. Bring to a boil, cover and simmer 1 hour. To serve, ladle into soup bowls and garnish with shredded cheese. Yield: 12 servings.

Note: If you don't like pressure cookers, simmer beef until tender and then follow directions.

Mexican Cornbread

1½ cups cornmeal
3 teaspoons baking powder
1 teaspoon salt
1 tablespoon sugar
¾ cup vegetable oil
1 cup cream-style corn
1 cup sour cream

3 eggs
2 tablespoons chopped pimentos
2 jalapeño peppers, chopped fine (optional)
½ onion, chopped fine
1 cup grated sharp cheese, divided

Mix together all ingredients, except cheese. Pour half of batter in well-greased baking dish or iron skillet. Top with ½ cup cheese. Add remaining batter and top with remaining cheese. Bake in a 350° oven 1 hour or until golden brown. Yield: 8 to 12 wedges.

Ooey Gooey Pumpkin Cake

CRUST:

1 box yellow cake mix

1 egg

1 stick butter, melted

Mix dry cake mix, egg and melted butter. Press into a 9x13-inch spray-coated pan.

FILLING:

1 (8-ounce) carton cream cheese, softened

1 (15-ounce) can pumpkin

3 eggs

1 stick butter, melted

1 teaspoon vanilla extract

1 teaspoon cinnamon

1 teaspoon nutmeg

3½ cups powdered sugar, unsifted

In a large mixing bowl, beat cream cheese and pumpkin until well blended. Add remaining ingredients and pour over Crust. Bake at 350° for 50 to 55 minutes or until well browned but the center still jiggles. Yield: 18 to 20 squares.

VARIATIONS:

GOOEY BUTTER CAKE

CRUST: Same as pumpkin version.

FILLING: Substitute with the following and bake as directed above.

1 (8-ounce) package cream cheese, softened

2 large eggs

1 stick butter, melted

1 teaspoon vanilla extract

3¾ cups powdered sugar

ALMOND GOOEY BUTTER CAKE

CRUST: Add ½ cup slivered almonds to recipe.

FILLING: Same as the Gooey Butter Cake filling variation, but substitute almond extract for vanilla. Bake as directed above.

CHOCOLATE MARBLE GOOEY BUTTER CAKE

CRUST: Same as pumpkin version.

FILLING: Add 1 cup semisweet chocolate chips to Gooey Butter Cake filling variation.

Cream Cheese Pound Cake

3 sticks butter, softened
1 (8-ounce) package cream cheese,
   softened
3 cups sugar
3 cups cake flour

6 large eggs
½ teaspoon vanilla extract
½ teaspoon lemon flavoring
½ teaspoon coconut flavoring

Cream butter and cream cheese until smooth; add sugar, 1 cup at a time, mixing until well blended. Alternate adding flour and eggs, mixing well after each addition. Stir in flavorings. Pour batter into a greased and floured Bundt pan. Bake at 340° for 50 minutes. Yield: 12 servings.

Christmas Dessert Extravaganza

Lemon Angel Bars

Turtles

Meringue Kisses

Amaretto Cream Napoleons

Fruitcake Cookies

Russian Tea Cakes

Ozark Mountain Bars

Date Pinwheel Cookies

Chinese Almond Cakes

Snickerdoodles

Triple Chocolate Chip Oatmeal Cookies

Raspberry Oatmeal Bars

Oatmeal-Coconut Cookies

Oatmeal Cranberry Walnut Cookies

Reese's Mini Peanut Butter Cup Cookies

Crisp Lemon Cookies

Fresh Coconut Cake (page 51)

Mom's Unusual Fruitcake (page 52)

German Chocolate Cake (page 94)

Bacardi Rum Cake (page 205)

Cinnamon Rum Cake (page 53)

Pumpkin Pie (page 50)

Layered Pumpkin Pie (page 203)

Bourbon Chocolate Chip Pecan Pie (page 50)

Lemon Angel Bars

1 box angel food cake mix   **1 (15.75-ounce) can lemon pie filling**

Stir together dry cake mix and lemon pie filling. Pour into ungreased 9x13-inch pan. Bake at 350° for 30 minutes or until top springs back when touched. Cool thoroughly.

FROSTING:

1 stick butter, softened   **1 (1-pound) box powdered sugar**
3 ounces cream cheese, softened   **Milk to moisten**

Cream together butter and cream cheese until fluffy. Gradually mix in powdered sugar until well blended. Add a small amount of milk to desired consistency. Frosting should be stiff but spreadable. Spread on cooled bars. Yield: 24 bars.

Turtles

1 (13-ounce) package caramels, wrappers   **3 cups pecan halves**
  removed   **Ghirardelli dark chocolate melting wafers**
2 tablespoons water   **(or any brand chocolate bark)**

Melt caramels in top of double boiler or in microwave with water. Stir in pecans. Drop by spoonfuls onto greased cookie sheet. Freeze 1 hour. Meanwhile, melt chocolate wafers. Dip caramel pieces into warm chocolate; remove to wax paper. Let cool and store in covered container. Yield: 36 turtles.

Meringue Kisses

2 egg whites   **Pinch salt**
¼ teaspoon cream of tartar   **½ teaspoon vanilla extract**
⅔ cup sugar   **Chocolate chips, optional**

Preheat oven to 350°. Beat first 5 ingredients in a medium-size bowl until stiff. Fold in chocolate chips, if desired. Spoon individual kisses onto an ungreased cookie sheet. Turn off oven. Place cookie sheet in oven 8 to 10 hours. Yield: 36 kisses.

Amaretto Cream Napoleons

1 (17.25-ounce package) or 2 sheets
   frozen puff pastry, thawed per package
   directions
1 (20-ounce) can evaporated milk
1½ cups sugar
5 tablespoons all-purpose flour

4 egg yolks
2 tablespoons butter
½ cup amaretto
1 teaspoon vanilla extract
1 teaspoon almond extract

Preheat oven to 400°. On lightly floured surface, cut pastry into 2x3-inch rectangles. Place on ungreased cookie sheet. Bake 18 to 20 minutes or until golden brown. Cool completely on wire rack.

In a medium saucepan, combine evaporated milk, sugar, flour, egg yolks and butter. Bring to a boil over medium heat, stirring constantly. Boil 2 to 3 minutes or until thickened. Remove from heat. Stir in amaretto and extracts. Cover and refrigerate until well chilled.

Carefully lift off tops of pastries. Generously spoon amaretto mixture on bottoms of pastries. Replace tops.

ICING:

2¼ cups sifted powdered sugar

3 tablespoons milk

Combine sugar and milk; stir until smooth. Generously spread icing on top of each pastry. Allow icing to harden.

DRIZZLE:

¼ cup semisweet chocolate chips

Place chocolate chips in a zip-close bag and set in a bowl of hot water to melt. Once melted, cut off a corner of the bag and drizzle on top of each pastry. Allow chocolate to harden. Store in an airtight container in refrigerator. Yield: about 2 dozen Napoleons (or more if you cut pastries into smaller rectangles).

Fruitcake Cookies

⅔ cup packed brown sugar
½ cup butter
1 egg
1 teaspoon vanilla extract
1 cup flour
½ teaspoon baking soda

Pinch salt
1 pound (2⅔ cups) chopped dates
1 cup fruitcake mix
½ cup candied cherries, chopped
1½ cups chopped assorted nuts (pecans, filberts, walnuts)

In large mixing bowl, cream together brown sugar and butter until light and fluffy. Add egg and vanilla; beat well. Stir together flour, baking soda and salt. Add to creamed mixture, beating until combined. Fold in fruits and nuts. Chill batter. Drop by tablespoonfuls onto greased cookie sheets. Bake at 325° for 12 minutes. Store baked cookies in airtight container overnight to soften. Yield: 4 dozen cookies.

Russian Tea Cakes

1 cup butter, softened
½ cup powdered sugar plus more for rolling cookies
1 teaspoon vanilla extract

¼ teaspoon salt
2¼ cups unbleached or all-purpose flour
¾ cup finely chopped nuts

In a large bowl, combine butter, powdered sugar, vanilla and salt on low speed of mixer about 1 minute until well blended. Gradually add flour at low speed until just combined. Stir in nuts.

Roll dough into 1-inch balls. Place about 1 inch apart on ungreased cookie sheet. Bake at 350° for 8 to 10 minutes until firm to the touch but not brown (do not overbake). While warm, roll in powdered sugar. Cool, roll again in powdered sugar before serving. Yield: 4 dozen cookies.

Ozark Mountain Bars

1 box yellow cake mix
1 cup light brown sugar
½ cup butter, melted
2 eggs

2 teaspoons vanilla extract
1 (6-ounce) package semisweet chocolate
    or butterscotch pieces
½ cup chopped pecans, optional

By hand or with mixer on low speed, combine all ingredients, adding chocolate pieces and nuts last. Beat well. Pour into greased 9x13-inch pan. Bake at 350° for 25 to 30 minutes. The cooked mixture is very chewy and may not look done, but it is. Cool and cut into bars. Yield: approximately 24 bars.

Date Pinwheel Cookies

DATE MIXTURE:

2 eggs, beaten
1½ cups chopped dates
½ cup sugar

½ cup water
¼ cup chopped nuts

In a saucepan, cook all ingredients together until thickened; set aside.

DOUGH:

1 cup shortening
1 cup sugar
1 cup brown sugar
1 teaspoon vanilla extract
1½ cups flour

1 teaspoon baking soda
1 teaspoon salt
3 cups quick-cooking oatmeal
½ cup chopped nuts
½ cup coconut

In a large bowl, mix together Dough ingredients until well blended. Separate into halves. Roll out dough (one half at a time) on a floured board. Spread half the Date Mixture on top of each. Lift with a spatula and roll like a jelly roll. Wrap in wax paper or plastic wrap. Chill until firm enough to slice.

Slice ¼-inch thick and bake on lightly greased cookie sheet at 350° until light brown, about 12 minutes. Dough may be frozen and baked later, or cookies make be frozen. Yield: approximately 6 dozen cookies.

Chinese Almond Cakes

¾ cup sugar
1 teaspoon baking powder
¼ teaspoon salt
¾ cup softened butter
1 egg

2 tablespoons water
1 teaspoon almond extract
2½ cups unbleached or all-purpose flour
⅓ cup whole almonds

In large bowl, beat first 7 ingredients with mixer on medium speed about 1 minute, blending well. Gradually add flour; blend at low speed until well mixed. Shape dough into 1-inch balls; place on greased cookie sheet about 2 inches apart. Flatten balls slightly with a glass dipped in sugar; press a whole almond firmly into the center of each cookie.

Bake at 350° for 8 to 12 minutes until firm to the touch but not brown (do not overbake). Immediately remove from cookie sheets; cool. Yield: 3 to 4 dozen cookies.

Snickerdoodles

1½ cups plus 3 tablespoons
   sugar, divided
½ cup butter, softened
½ cup shortening
2 eggs

2¾ cups flour
2 teaspoons cream of tartar
1 teaspoon baking soda
¼ teaspoon salt
3 teaspoons ground cinnamon

Cream together 1½ cups sugar, butter, shortening and eggs. Combine flour, cream of tartar, baking soda and salt; add to creamed mixture, mixing until well blended. Shape dough into 1-inch balls and roll the top of each ball in mixture of cinnamon and remaining 3 tablespoons sugar. (Do not roll bottom of ball in cinnamon and sugar due to possible overbaking.) Place balls top side up on ungreased cookie sheet. Bake at 400° for 8 to 10 minutes. Cool and store in covered container. Yield: 4 dozen cookies.

Triple Chocolate Chip Oatmeal Cookies

1 cup butter, softened
1 cup sugar
1 cup brown sugar
2 eggs
1 teaspoon vanilla extract
2 cups flour
2½ cups quick-cooking oatmeal

½ teaspoon salt
1 teaspoon baking powder
1 teaspoon baking soda
6 ounces milk chocolate chips
6 ounces semisweet chocolate chips
6 ounces white chocolate chips

Cream first 5 ingredients until light and fluffy. Mix next 5 ingredients and add to creamed mixture. Stir in all chocolate chips. Roll into ping-pong-size balls. Bake on ungreased cookie sheet in 375° oven 8 to 10 minutes. Do not overbake. Yield: approximately 6½ dozen cookies.

Raspberry Oatmeal Bars

1 box deluxe yellow cake mix
2½ cups quick-cooking oats
1½ sticks butter, melted

1 cup raspberry preserves or jam
1 tablespoon water

Preheat oven to 375°. Grease a 9x13-inch pan. Combine dry cake mix and oats in large bowl; add melted butter and stir until crumbly. Measure half of crumb mixture (about 3 cups) into pan. Press firmly to cover bottom. Combine preserves and water until well blended. Spread over crumb mixture in pan. Sprinkle remaining crumb mixture over preserves; pat firmly to make top even. Bake at 375° for 18 to 23 minutes or until very light brown. Cool in pan on rack; cut into bars. Store in airtight container. Yield: 4 dozen bars.

Note: Apricot, blackberry, or strawberry preserves can be substituted.

Oatmeal-Coconut Cookies

1 cup shortening, melted
1 cup all-purpose flour
1 cup sugar
1 cup brown sugar
4 cups rolled oats

1 cup coconut
½ teaspoon salt
1 teaspoon baking soda
2 eggs, beaten
1 teaspoon vanilla extract

Combine first 8 ingredients. Add beaten eggs and vanilla. Mix by hand until well blended. Form into walnut-size balls and place on greased cookie sheets. Bake at 325° for 8 to 10 minutes. Let cool before removing from cookie sheet. Yield: approximately 4 to 5 dozen cookies.

Oatmeal Cranberry Walnut Cookies

¾ cup sugar
¼ cup packed brown sugar
½ cup butter, softened
½ teaspoon vanilla extract
1 egg
¾ cup flour

½ teaspoon baking soda
½ teaspoon cinnamon
¼ teaspoon salt
1½ cups quick-cooking oats
1 cup Craisins
1 cup chopped walnuts

Preheat oven to 375°. Grease cookie sheets. In large mixing bowl, beat sugars and butter until light and fluffy. Add vanilla and egg; blend well. Stir in flour, baking soda, cinnamon and salt; mix well. Stir in oats, Craisins and walnuts. Drop by rounded teaspoonfuls onto cookie sheets 2 inches apart. Bake at 375° for 7 to 10 minutes or until edges are light, golden brown. Cool 1 minute; remove from cookie sheets. Yield: approximately 3½ dozen cookies.

Reese's Mini Peanut Butter Cup Cookies

1 cup butter-flavor Crisco
¾ cup sugar
¾ cup packed brown sugar
¾ cup Peter Pan peanut butter
1½ teaspoons vanilla extract
1 teaspoon water
2 eggs

2¼ cups all-purpose flour
1 teaspoon baking powder
1 teaspoon salt
1 (8-ounce) package Reese's mini peanut butter cups (not miniatures but minis)
1 cup milk chocolate chips (or 1 cup Reese's peanut butter chips)

Beat Crisco, sugars, peanut butter, vanilla and water in a large mixing bowl at medium speed until well blended. Add eggs and beat until blended. Combine flour, baking powder and salt and gradually add to creamed mixture until blended using low speed on mixer. Stir in Reese's minis and chips. Drop by rounded tablespoonfuls onto a greased or parchment paper-lined cookie sheet 2 inches apart. Bake at 350° for 10 to 12 minutes or until light golden brown. Remove to cooling rack. Yield: 3½ to 4 dozen cookies.

Crisp Lemon Cookies

1⅓ cups butter, softened
2 cups powdered sugar
2 tablespoons lemon juice
2 teaspoons grated lemon peel

½ teaspoon vanilla extract
3 cups all-purpose flour
¼ cup sugar
¾ cup vanilla or white chips, melted

In a large mixing bowl, cream butter and powdered sugar until light and fluffy. Beat in lemon juice, lemon peel and vanilla. Gradually add flour and mix well. Shape dough into 1-inch balls. Place on ungreased baking sheets 2 inches apart. Coat the bottom of a flat-bottom glass with cooking spray; dip in sugar. Flatten cookies with glass, redipping in sugar as needed.

Bake at 325° for 11 to 13 minutes until edges are lightly browned. Remove to wire racks to cool. Drizzle with melted vanilla chips. Yield: 4½ dozen cookies.

Note: I melt the chips in a zip-close bag, and cut off one corner to drizzle.

Christmas Dinner

Overnight Fruit Ambrosia

Rotisserie Turkey

Giblet Gravy

Cornbread Dressing (page 201)

Rutabagas

Corn Casserole

Sweet Potato Casserole

Serve With:
Mashed Potatoes
Peas with Mushrooms
Dinner Rolls

Bourbon Chocolate Chip Pecan Pie

Pumpkin Pie

Fresh Coconut Cake

Mom's Unusual Fruitcake

Cinnamon Rum Cake

This Christmas menu was assembled with everyone in mind—you, the cook, family, and friends. You can now enjoy these occasions and not feel weary from the preparations, since everything can be prepared ahead. Dishes can literally go from refrigerator to oven to table. You can relax and enjoy the day and the meal while impressing your guests.

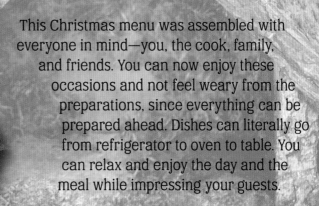

Overnight Fruit Ambrosia

2¼ cups miniature marshmallows
1 (20-ounce) can pineapple chunks, drained
1 (11-ounce) can mandarin orange sections, drained
1 (3.5-ounce) package coconut flakes
1 pint (16 ounces) sour cream
¼ teaspoon salt

Mix all ingredients and chill overnight. Stir and serve. Yield: 6 to 8 servings.

Rotisserie Turkey

You can bake your turkey, if you prefer. For oven-roasted turkey,
deep-fried or smoked brined recipes, see page 199.

1 (12- to 14-pound) turkey

Defrost turkey in refrigerator 3 days if frozen. Remove giblets and neck (reserve giblets for gravy). Wash bird and pat dry. Roast turkey according to rotisserie instructions. Yield: 12 to 14 servings.

Giblet Gravy

Reserved giblets from turkey
Salt and pepper to taste
1 (14-ounce) can chicken broth
1 chicken bouillon cube
¼ cup flour
½ cup water

Season giblets (neck, liver, gizzard and heart) with salt and pepper. Place in saucepan, add water to cover and cook until done. Remove giblets; cool and chop. Add broth and bouillon cube to giblet liquid. Mix flour and ½ cup water until smooth. Pour mixture through a strainer into the hot liquid. Stir until thickened and add chopped giblets. Yield: 2 cups.

Rutabagas

These were a must for my daddy. He was born and raised outside of Boston, Massachusetts. I guess this is a Yankee thing.

2 to 3 firm, medium-size rutabagas　　　**Butter to taste**

Peel rutabagas and cut into pieces. I cook these in a pressure cooker 10 minutes; otherwise, boil until tender. Pour off liquid and mash with butter. Yield: 6 to 8 servings.

Corn Casserole

1 (15.25-ounce) can whole-kernel corn　　　**1 cup oil**
1 (14.75-ounce) can cream-style corn　　　**4 eggs, beaten**
½ teaspoon garlic powder　　　**1 (2-ounce) jar diced pimentos**
1 cup white cornmeal mix　　　**Grated cheese to cover**

Mix all ingredients together except cheese and put in a casserole dish coated with cooking spray. Cover with cheese. Bake at 350° for 45 minutes. This resembles a soufflé and warms over nicely. Yield: 6 to 8 servings.

Sweet Potato Casserole

4 sweet potatoes, peeled, boiled and　　　1 teaspoon cinnamon
**　mashed**　　　**½ teaspoon nutmeg**
½ cup orange juice　　　**½ teaspoon salt**
½ cup brown sugar　　　**Miniature marshmallows**
2 tablespoons butter, melted

Mix all ingredients together and pour into a casserole dish coated with cooking spray. Bake at 350° for 25 minutes. (If refrigerated overnight, bake 40 minutes.) Remove from oven and cover top of casserole with marshmallows. Place under broiler until golden brown; watch constantly to avoid burning. Yield: 10 to 12 servings.

Note: May substitute 1 large can sweet potatoes or yams, drained and mashed.

Bourbon Chocolate Chip Pecan Pie

½ cup chopped pecans	¾ cup pancake syrup
3 tablespoons bourbon	1 teaspoon vanilla extract
¼ cup butter, melted	Pinch salt
1 cup sugar	½ cup chocolate chips
3 eggs, slightly beaten	1 (9-inch) pie shell, unbaked

Soak pecans in bourbon and set aside. In a bowl, beat butter, sugar and eggs until fluffy. Blend in syrup, vanilla and salt. Add chocolate chips. Pour filling into unbaked pie shell and arrange pecans on top. Bake at 375° for 45 to 55 minutes. Cool before slicing. Serve with whipped topping if desired. Yield: 8 servings.

Pumpkin Pie

¾ cup sugar	2 large eggs
½ teaspoon salt	1 (15-ounce) can pure pumpkin
1 teaspoon cinnamon	1 (12-ounce) can evaporated milk
½ teaspoon ground ginger	1 (9-inch) deep-dish pie shell, unbaked
¼ teaspoon ground cloves	

Mix sugar, salt, cinnamon, ginger and cloves in a small bowl. Beat eggs in a large bowl. Stir in pumpkin and sugar-spice mixture. Gradually stir in evaporated milk. Pour into pie shell. Bake in preheated 425° oven 15 minutes. Reduce temperature to 350°; bake 45 to 50 minutes or until knife inserted near center comes out clean. Cool on wire rack 2 hours. Serve immediately or refrigerate. Yield: 8 servings.

Fresh Coconut Cake

The coconut cake is the "Grand Dame" of all cakes. My mother made this cake every Christmas with fresh coconut. Frozen coconut is just as good, and much easier.

1 cup Crisco shortening	4 teaspoons baking powder
2 cups sugar	½ teaspoon salt
1 teaspoon vanilla extract	1 cup milk
3 cups cake flour	8 egg whites, stiffly beaten

Cream shortening with sugar; add vanilla. Combine flour, baking powder and salt. Alternately add milk and flour mixture to creamed mixture. Fold in beaten egg whites. Line bottom of 3 (9-inch) cake pans with wax paper and distribute batter evenly in pans. Bake at 350° for 30 to 40 minutes. Cool before frosting.

SEVEN-MINUTE WHITE FROSTING:

2 egg whites, unbeaten	1½ teaspoons light corn syrup
1½ cups sugar	1 teaspoon vanilla extract
5 tablespoons cold water	Fresh or frozen grated coconut
¼ teaspoon cream of tartar	

Combine egg whites, sugar, cold water, cream of tartar and corn syrup in top of a double boiler over rapidly boiling water. Beat constantly 7 minutes. Remove from heat. Add vanilla; continue beating until spreading consistency. Frost tops of each layer, including the top layer, and sprinkle with coconut. Assemble cake and frost sides; garnish with coconut.

Mom's Unusual Fruitcake

This cake was always a treat for my daddy and me. We
need to name it something else so people will try it.
Ignore the fruitcake stigma and try this cake.

3 cups sifted cake flour
2¼ cups sugar
2¼ teaspoons baking soda
2¼ teaspoons salt
3 tablespoons cocoa
¾ teaspoon each: cinnamon, cloves,
   nutmeg, allspice

¾ cup Crisco shortening
2¼ cups unsweetened applesauce
3 eggs, unbeaten
¾ cup each: raisins, currants and dates,
   cut in small pieces
1 cup candied fruitcake mix
1 cup chopped walnuts or pecans, toasted

Sift flour, sugar, baking soda, salt, cocoa and spices into mixing bowl. Drop in Crisco. Add applesauce; beat 200 strokes (2 minutes by hand or with mixer set at low speed). Add eggs and beat 200 strokes. Add fruits and nuts. Mix thoroughly. Bake in Crisco-coated and floured 8½-inch tube pan at 350° for 1 hour and 25 to 30 minutes. Spread with Cranberry Cream Icing, if desired. This cake is good without frosting.

CRANBERRY CREAM ICING:

2 tablespoons Crisco shortening
1 tablespoon butter, softened
1 teaspoon vanilla extract
¼ teaspoon salt

3 tablespoons cranberry juice
3 cups powdered sugar
1 tablespoon light cream, scalded

Cream together the Crisco, butter, vanilla and salt. Alternately add cranberry juice and powdered sugar. Add scalded cream; stir till spreading consistency.

Cinnamon Rum Cake

1 package moist yellow cake mix
½ cup sugar
¾ cup vegetable oil
5 eggs

1 cup sour cream
1 cup chopped pecans
1 tablespoon cinnamon
2 tablespoons brown sugar

Preheat oven to 350°. Grease and flour a tube or Bundt pan. Combine dry cake mix, sugar, oil, eggs and sour cream. Blend with electric mixer at low speed until ingredients are moistened. Beat at medium speed 2 minutes. Stir in pecans. Pour half of batter into prepared pan. Combine cinnamon and brown sugar. Sprinkle over batter. Pour remaining batter into pan. Bake 45 minutes or until a toothpick inserted in cake comes out clean. Allow cake to cool 10 minutes. Prepare Rum Sauce and pour over cake in pan. Cool at least 1½ hours before turning out of pan. Yield: 12 servings.

RUM SAUCE:

1 cup sugar
¼ cup water

½ cup rum

In small saucepan, combine sugar and water. Cook over high heat, stirring to dissolve sugar, and bring liquid to a boil. Add rum, stir to mix, and remove from heat. Allow to cool slightly and pour over warm cake in pan.

Gift Basket Jams

Carrot Cake Jam

Sweet Cherry, Peach Brandy, and Strawberry Amaretto Jam

Mom's Apple Pie in a Jar

Strawberry Margarita Preserves

For friends and associates, I make Christmas baskets every year that include an assortment of jams and preserves along with crackers, baking mixes, and festive cookies and candies. The recipes here are perfect for creating baskets for your friends, family and work associates.

Carrot Cake Jam

1½ cups finely grated, peeled carrots

1½ cups peeled, cored and chopped pears

1¾ cups canned crushed pineapple, including juice

3 tablespoons lemon juice

1 teaspoon ground cinnamon

½ teaspoon nutmeg

½ teaspoon ground cloves

1 (1.75-ounce) package regular powdered fruit pectin

6½ cups sugar

Prepare 6 (8-ounce) canning jars and lids by sterilizing in boiling water; remove.

In large, deep stainless steel saucepan (I use a stainless steel Dutch oven), combine carrots, pears, pineapple with juice, lemon juice, cinnamon, nutmeg and cloves. Bring to a boil over high heat, stirring frequently. Reduce heat, cover, and boil gently 20 minutes, stirring occasionally. Remove from heat and whisk in pectin until dissolved. Bring to a boil over high heat, stirring frequently. Add sugar all at once and return to a full rolling boil, stirring constantly. Boil hard, stirring constantly 1 minute. Remove from heat and skim off foam.

Ladle hot jam into hot jars, leaving ¼-inch headspace. Remove air bubbles and adjust headspace if necessary by adding hot jam. Wipe rim. Center lid on jar and screw band down until resistance is met; then increase to fingertip tight.

Use this inverted method to seal: Turn jars upside down in a draft-free area 5 minutes and then turn the jars right side up. You will begin to hear a popping sound after a few minutes as the jars seal. Yield: 6 (8-ounce) jars.

Sweet Cherry Jam

The alcohol cooks out, leaving an awesome flavor which gives it a gourmet flair.

4 cups chopped pitted sweet cherries
4 tablespoons lemon juice
½ teaspoon ground cinnamon
½ teaspoon ground cloves

¼ cup black cherry brandy
1 (1.75-ounce) package powered fruit pectin
5 cups sugar (pre-measure)

Prepare 6 or 7 (8-ounce) canning jars and lids by sterilizing in boiling water; remove.

Combine cherries, lemon juice, cinnamon, cloves and brandy in a large, deep stainless steel saucepan or Dutch oven. Make sure the pan fits your heating element and is flat on the bottom for even heating. Whisk in pectin until dissolved. Bring to a boil over high heat, stirring frequently. Add sugar all at once and return to a full rolling boil, stirring constantly. Boil hard, stirring constantly, 1 minute. Remove from heat; skim off foam.

Ladle hot jam into hot jars, leaving ¼-inch headspace. Remove air bubbles by sliding a rubber spatula between the jar and food; add more hot jam if necessary. Wipe rim and center lid on jar. Screw bands down until fingertip tight.

Use the inverted method to seal as described on previous page, or follow these steps for water bath method: Place jars in canner, making sure the jars are completely covered with water. Place the lid on canner, bring to a boil and process 10 minutes. Remove canner lid, wait 5 minutes and remove jars. Lids will pop when sealed. Let cool overnight; then store in a cool, dry, dark place.

VARIATIONS: These are just a few ideas. Feel free to try substitutions to suit your taste.

Peach Brandy Jam
SUBSTITUTE: **4 cups chopped, peeled, pitted peaches** for the cherries
SUBSTITUTE: **1 teaspoon nutmeg** for the cinnamon and cloves
SUBSTITUTE: **¼ cup peach brandy or peach schnapps** for the black cherry brandy

Strawberry Amaretto Jam
SUBSTITUTE: **4 cups chopped, hulled strawberries** for the cherries
SUBSTITUTE: **1 teaspoon cinnamon** for the cinnamon and cloves
SUBSTITUTE: **¼ cup amaretto** for the black cherry brandy

Mom's Apple Pie in a Jar

¾ cup raisins (or dried cranberries)
6 cups chopped, cored, and peeled Granny Smith apples (or other tart apples)
1 lemon, juiced and rind grated for zest
1 cup unsweetened apple juice
1 (1.75-ounce) package regular powdered fruit pectin
9 cups sugar
1 teaspoon ground cinnamon
½ teaspoon ground nutmeg

Prepare 6 (8-ounce) canning jars and lids by sterilizing in boiling water; remove.

Pulse raisins until finely chopped in a food processor and set aside.

In a large, deep stainless steel saucepan (I use a stainless steel Dutch oven) combine apples, lemon juice, lemon zest and apple juice. Bring to a boil over high heat, stirring frequently. Reduce heat and boil gently, stirring occasionally, until apples begin to soften, about 10 minutes. Remove from heat and whisk in pectin until dissolved. Stir in chopped raisins. Return to high heat and bring to a boil, stirring frequently. Add sugar all at once, and return to a full rolling boil, stirring constantly. Boil hard, stirring constantly, 1 minute. Remove from heat, and stir in cinnamon and nutmeg. Skim off foam.

Ladle hot jam into hot jars, leaving ¼-inch headspace. Remove air bubbles and adjust headspace, if necessary. Wipe rim, center lid on jar and screw band down until resistance is met. Increase to fingertip tight.

Turn the jar upside down in a draft-free area 5 minutes and then turn the jar right side up. You will begin to hear a popping sound after a few minutes as the jars seal. Yield: 6 (8-ounce) jar.

Strawberry Margarita Preserves

This also makes a great cheesecake topping.

6 cups quartered hulled strawberries
2 cups peeled, cored and chopped tart apples
¼ cup lemon juice
4 cups sugar
½ cup tequila
½ cup orange-flavored liqueur
2 tablespoons strawberry schnapps, optional

Prepare 6 (8-ounce) canning jars and lids by sterilizing in boiling water; remove.

In a large, deep stainless steel saucepan, combine strawberries, apples and lemon juice. Bring to a boil over high heat, stirring constantly. Add sugar, stirring until dissolved. Reduce heat and boil gently, stirring frequently, until mixture thickens—about 25 minutes. Test the syrup for gel by placing a small amount on a cold dish and see if it gels. When it gels, add the tequila, liqueur and schnapps, if using. Return to medium-high heat and bring to a boil, stirring constantly. Boil hard, stirring constantly, 5 minutes. Remove from heat and skim off foam.

Ladle hot jam into hot jars, leaving ¼-inch headspace. Remove air bubbles and adjust headspace, if necessary, by adding hot jam. Wipe rim, center lid on jar and screw band down until resistance is met. Increase to fingertip tight. Invert jars (turn jars upside down) 5 minutes. Then turn right side up and listen for the pop signaling the jars are sealing. Yield: 6 (8-ounce) jars.

New Year's Eve Celebration

Show-Stopping Torte
Marinated Tomato and Mozzarella Salad
Broiled Marinated Steak
Burgundy Mushrooms
Loaded Baked Potatoes
Spinach for Men
Bananas Foster
Upside-Down Bananas Foster Cake

Show-Stopping Torte

2 (8-ounce) packages cream cheese, softened, divided
1½ tablespoons Durkee mustard-mayonnaise sauce, divided
4 ounces shredded sharp Cheddar cheese
½ (7-ounce) can crushed pineapple, drained
¼ cup green onions, chopped
1 teaspoon dried mint
¾ cup chopped pecans
¾ cup orange marmalade, divided
1½ teaspoons mayonnaise
1 tablespoon dried orange peel
1½ teaspoons orange extract
Toasted pecan halves for garnish

FIRST LAYER:

Process 1 package cream cheese, ¾ tablespoon mustard-mayonnaise sauce, Cheddar cheese, pineapple, green onions and mint in a food processor until blended, stopping to scrape down sides. Press into bottom of a plastic wrap-lined 9-inch springform pan and sprinkle with chopped pecans.

SECOND LAYER:

Process remaining package of cream cheese, remaining ¾ tablespoon mustard-mayonnaise sauce, ⅔ cup orange marmalade, mayonnaise, orange peel and orange extract in food processor until smooth, stopping to scrape down sides. Spread over first layer, pressing until smooth. Cover and chill up to 3 days. Remove from pan; spread with remaining marmalade. Garnish with toasted pecan halves. Serve with gingersnaps. Yield: approximately 15 appetizer servings.

Note: To toast pecans, bake in a shallow pan at 300°, stirring occasionally, 7 to 10 minutes or until lightly toasted. Cool.

Marinated Tomato and Mozzarella Salad

½ pound fresh mozzarella cheese
3 large red tomatoes, sliced
½ teaspoon salt

Kraft Italian pesto dressing
½ cup chopped fresh basil
Freshly ground black pepper

Cut cheese into 12 slices; sprinkle tomato slices evenly with salt. Alternate tomato and cheese slices on a platter; drizzle with dressing. Cover and chill 4 hours. Just before serving, arrange on lettuce leaves and sprinkle with basil and pepper. Yield: 6 servings.

Broiled Marinated Steak

½ (8-ounce) bottle RealLime juice
1 (5-ounce) bottle soy sauce

Your favorite cut of steak

Mix lime juice and soy sauce. Marinate steak several hours in refrigerator, turning occasionally. Grill or broil steak to desired doneness. (Men love these steaks!)

Burgundy Mushrooms

I really love these, so I double the recipe.

1 pound fresh mushrooms
½ cup coarsely chopped onion
2 tablespoons butter
½ cup Burgundy (or other dry red wine)

½ cup beef broth
1 tablespoon Worcestershire sauce
¼ teaspoon salt
⅛ teaspoon pepper

Clean mushrooms with damp paper towels; cut in half. Sauté mushrooms and onion in butter in a large skillet over medium-high heat 3 minutes. Combine Burgundy and remaining ingredients; add to skillet. Cook over medium-high heat 15 minutes or until most of liquid evaporates. Serve hot. Yield: 4 to 6 generous servings.

Loaded Baked Potatoes

Medium-size baking potatoes (1 for each guest)
Toppings: Butter, shredded cheese of any kind, sour cream, bacon bits, chives

Pierce potatoes with a fork and microwave 5 minutes for each potato (microwaves vary). Wrap in foil and place in warm oven or slow cooker to hold until ready to serve. Top with butter, shredded cheese, sour cream, bacon bits and chives.

Spinach for Men

Men love this dish!

1 to 2 (10-ounce) packages frozen chopped spinach
½ to 1 (8-ounce) jar Cheez Whiz
1 to 2 tablespoons salsa (or picante sauce) to taste

Cook spinach according to package directions, drain. Add Cheez Whiz and salsa. Stir and serve. Yield: 4 to 8 servings.

Bananas Foster

This is a fun and flavorful New Orleans classic, easy skillet dessert.

¼ cup butter
⅓ cup firmly packed brown sugar
½ teaspoon ground cinnamon
4 firm bananas, quartered

⅓ cup banana liqueur
⅓ cup dark or light rum
1 pint vanilla ice cream

Melt butter in a large skillet over medium-high heat. Add brown sugar, cinnamon, bananas and liqueur. Cook, stirring constantly, 2 minutes or until bananas are tender. Pour rum into a small, long-handled saucepan; heat just until warm. Remove from heat. Ignite with a long match and pour over bananas. Baste bananas with sauce until flames die down. Serve immediately over ice cream. Yield: 4 servings. (Double recipe for a party.)

Upside-Down Bananas Foster Cake

If Bananas Foster's preparation is of concern to you, here is a delicious, easy substitute.

TOPPING:

⅓ cup butter
1 cup packed light brown sugar
½ teaspoon cinnamon
2 tablespoons light rum
3 cups sliced bananas, cut on the diagonal about ⅓ inch thick (3 large bananas)

Melt butter in cast-iron skillet over low heat. Remove from heat and, using a fork, stir in brown sugar, cinnamon and rum. Spread mixture evenly over bottom of skillet and arrange the bananas on top to cover.

CAKE:

1 package butter recipe golden cake mix
1 stick butter, melted
1½ cups whole milk
2 large eggs
4 teaspoons fresh lemon juice

Place dry cake mix, melted butter, milk, eggs, and lemon juice in a large mixing bowl. Blend on low speed 1 minute; scrape down the sides with a spatula. Increase mixer speed to medium and beat an additional 2 minutes. Batter should look creamy.

Pour batter on top of bananas in the skillet, smoothing to cover all bananas. Bake in 350° oven for to 45 minutes. Cake should rise and spring back when lightly pressed with finger. Remove cake from oven and run knife around the skillet. Carefully invert onto a heat-proof serving plate. This cake is best served warm with vanilla ice cream or whipped cream.

New Year's Day Soul Food Bonanza

Creamy Coleslaw

Super Easy Coleslaw

Hoppin' John (Black-eyed Peas)

Sautéed Cabbage

Southern-Style Collards

Serve With:
Fluffy Rice or Chicken Rice-A-Roni

Cornbread

Dr. Bird Cake

We in the South have many traditions. One tradition is that what we eat New Year's Day sets the stage for the rest of the year. Black-eyed peas are sure to bring good luck, and cabbage means you will have money. My family always eats these two items on New Year's Day. You might notice that this menu has a double dose of cabbage. My daughter, Lyndsey, will not eat sautéed cabbage, but she loves coleslaw. The slaw adds great texture and color to this menu and I give you two recipes to choose from. I don't think anyone would mind a double helping of money this year.

Creamy Coleslaw

½ cup mayonnaise
½ cup sour cream
2 tablespoons sugar
2 tablespoons white vinegar
1 teaspoon celery seed
¼ teaspoon mustard seed
½ teaspoon salt
½ teaspoon paprika
¼ teaspoon pepper
¼ cup diced onion, optional
1 (14-ounce) package chopped coleslaw

Combine all ingredient except coleslaw. Pour mixture over coleslaw; toss and chill before serving. Yield: 4 to 6 servings.

Super Easy Coleslaw

If you want a coleslaw that is super easy, here is the one for you.

½ cup mayonnaise
¼ cup Briannas' blush wine vinaigrette
1 (14-ounce) package chopped coleslaw

Combine mayonnaise and vinaigrette and pour over coleslaw, and mix well. Refrigerate if not serving immediately. Yield: 4 to 6 servings.

Hoppin' John (Black-Eyed Peas)

1 (1-pound) package dried black-eyed peas, soaked overnight in water to cover
4 cups water
2 teaspoons salt
¼ teaspoon pepper
1 tablespoon minced onion
2 stalks celery, cut in half
1 pound Hillshire Farm sausage, cut into links

Drain soaked black-eyed peas and place in a slow cooker. Add remaining ingredients, except sausage. Cover, and cook on high 1 to 2 hours, and then on low 8 to 9 hours. Add sausage around the sides of the slow cooker the last hour of cooking. Serve over Minute Rice prepared according to package directions or cornbread. Yield: 4 to 6 servings.

Sautéed Cabbage

½ stick butter
1 head cabbage, sliced
1 teaspoon salt
¼ teaspoon pepper

Melt butter in skillet. Add cabbage and stir-fry until slightly tender. Stir in salt and pepper; serve. Yield: 4 to 6 servings.

Southern-Style Collards

1 bunch collard greens (about 3 pounds)
1 pound smoked ham hocks
1½ quarts water
¼ teaspoon salt
Pepper sauce or vinegar, optional

Remove pulpy stems and discolored spots on leaves of greens and discard. Wash greens thoroughly; drain and chop. Combine ham hocks and water in a Dutch oven; bring to a boil. Reduce heat and simmer, partially covered, 45 minutes or until meat is tender. Remove ham hocks; add salt and greens to pan. Simmer, uncovered, 45 minutes or until greens are tender, adding more water if necessary. Serve with pepper sauce of choice or vinegar. Yield: 6 servings.

Cornbread

2 cups self-rising cornmeal
1 tablespoon sugar
1 large egg, beaten
1¾ cups milk or buttermilk
¼ cup vegetable oil

Combine cornmeal and sugar in a bowl. Add egg, milk, and oil. Stir until moist. Place a well-greased 9-inch iron skillet in preheated 450° oven 5 minutes. Carefully remove from oven and pour batter into skillet. Bake at 450° for 20 to 25 minutes or until golden brown. Yield: 4 to 6 servings.

Dr. Bird Cake

The Dr. Bird Cake is the basic Hummingbird cake batter
baked in a Bundt pan and served with no frosting.

3 cups sifted flour
1 teaspoon baking soda
1 teaspoon cinnamon
2 cups sugar
1 teaspoon salt

1 cup cooking oil
1 (8-ounce) can crushed pineapple
1½ teaspoons vanilla extract
3 eggs
2 cups diced ripe bananas

Sift dry ingredients into a large bowl. Add oil, pineapple and juice, vanilla and eggs to dry ingredients. Stir to blend. Do not beat! Fold in diced bananas. Pour into a greased Bundt pan and bake at 350° for 1 hour and 15 minutes. Cool before removing from pan. Serve plain or with whipped cream or ice cream. Yield: 16 servings.

Valentine Dinner

Drunken Pork Chops and Sliced Sweet Potatoes
Green Bean Bundles
Artichoke Bake
Cashew Shrimp Salad
Chocolate Covered Cherry Cake

My family and I traveled to the Big Island of Hawaii several years ago, and this entrée was one that my husband ordered for dinner one evening. It is very good, and don't be shy about the sweet potatoes. I don't eat sweet potatoes normally, but this is a very tasty combination that your friends will enjoy.

Drunken Pork Chops and Sliced Sweet Potatoes

SWEET BOURBON MARINADE:

¼ cup pineapple juice

2 tablespoons soy sauce

2 tablespoons brown sugar

1 teaspoon bourbon

¼ teaspoon pepper

⅛ teaspoon garlic powder

½ cup vegetable oil

2 teaspoons chopped chives, optional

Combine all ingredients, reserve ¼ cup for cooking purposes. Yield: ¾ cup.

6 boneless pork chops, ¼-inch to ½-inch thick
Butter

Marinate pork chops 3 to 4 hours in ½ cup Sweet Bourbon Marinade.

Remove pork from marinade and sauté pork chops in butter until brown. Remove chops from pan and add reserved ¼ cup marinade to skillet, scraping bottom of pan. Reduce heat and return chops to pan. Cover and cook until done. Remove chops and keep warm.

2 large sweet potatoes, sliced or julienned

At this point, increase the heat in pan, add sweet potatoes and stir-fry in marinade. Cover and cook on low heat to desired doneness. Some people like the potatoes crunchy, and some like them soft but still holding their shape.

To serve, plate the pork chops and potatoes with Green Bean Bundles (see next page), and garnish with fruits of choice.

Green Bean Bundles

2 (15-ounce) cans vertical-packed green beans or 1 pound fresh green beans, blanched
½ pound bacon, cut in half

Drain beans. Divide into bundles of approximately 5 beans each. Wrap each bundle in ½ slice of bacon and secure with a toothpick. Broil on a rack until the bacon is cooked.

SAUCE:

3 tablespoons butter
3 tablespoons tarragon vinegar
½ teaspoon salt

1 teaspoon paprika
1 tablespoon chopped fresh parsley
1 teaspoon onion juice

Combine butter, vinegar, salt, paprika, parsley and onion juice; simmer until hot. Pour over cooked bean bundles and serve. Beans and Sauce may be prepared ahead of time and refrigerated. Broil bean bundles and reheat sauce at serving time. Yield: 8 servings.

Note: If you prefer a sweeter flavor, use Glaze instead of Sauce. My family likes these even without any sauce.

GLAZE:

¾ stick butter
½ cup brown sugar

⅛ teaspoon garlic powder
Salt and pepper to taste

Melt butter and add sugar, garlic powder, salt and pepper. Place bean bundles in a baking dish. Drizzle Glaze over bean bundles. Bake at 375° about 45 minutes or until bacon is cooked. Watch carefully toward end as beans tend to burn quickly.

Artichoke Bake

1 (14-ounce) can artichoke hearts
1 cup grated Parmesan cheese
¾ cup mayonnaise

1 clove garlic, minced
¼ teaspoon Worcestershire sauce
⅛ teaspoon hot sauce

Combine all ingredients, stirring well. Spoon into a lightly greased 1-quart casserole dish and bake, uncovered, at 350° for 20 minutes or until bubbly. Serve with melba toast rounds. Yield: 2 cups.

Cashew Shrimp Salad

1 cup V8 juice
1 tablespoon soy sauce
1 teaspoon vegetable oil
½ teaspoon grated lemon peel
½ teaspoon grated ginger (or 1 teaspoon ground ginger)
1 pound shrimp, cooked, shelled and deveined
1½ cups cucumber slices
1 cup matchstick carrots
3 green onions sliced (½ cup)
¼ cup chopped dry roasted unsalted cashews (1 ounce)
Butterhead lettuce leaves
Cashews, if desired

In medium bowl, combine juice, soy sauce, oil, lemon peel and ginger. Add shrimp, cucumbers, carrots and onions. Toss and coat well. Cover and refrigerate until serving time, at least 2 hours. Before serving, add cashews and toss to coat well. To serve, place on lettuce-lined plates and arrange shrimp mixture on top. Garnish with whole cashews.

Chocolate Covered Cherry Cake

1 package devil's food cake with pudding
1 (21-ounce) can cherry pie filling
1 teaspoon almond or vanilla extract
2 large eggs
1 (16-ounce) can prepared chocolate frosting

Combine the first 4 ingredients in a bowl and stir until blended. Pour into a greased and floured 9x13-inch pan and bake at 350° for 30 to 35 minutes. Center should spring back when touched. Cool and then frost with prepared frosting.

Lenten Fellowship Dinners

Several years ago, my church developed fellowship dinners that we called Cell Groups. We meet every Sunday during the Lenten season for Bible study. Lent is a journey in which we walk with Jesus to the cross.

Our group enjoys fellowship so much that we decided to meet on Sunday evenings and combine Bible study with a potluck dinner. We carry this tradition from year to year. Our weekly potlucks feature different types of food such as Mexican, German, Italian, French, and Oriental.

The following section includes these fellowship potluck dinners. We have great cooks in our group, and we hope you enjoy these recipes!

You can pick and choose from these potluck recipes to create your own unique menus even adding your own favorite recipes. Use the themes as a guideline for a great party dinner. Go ahead—have some fun!

Mexican Lenten Dinner

Mexican Layered Dip

Green Chile and Cheese Dip

Santa Fe Soup

Mexican Quiche

Tortilla Casserole

Spanish Rice

Chicken Tortilla

Chili and Enchiladas

Mexican Chocolate Sheet Cake

Strawberry Margarita

Preserves (page 59)

Mexican Layered Dip

1 (8-ounce) package cream cheese, softened
1 (16-ounce) can chili beans, drained
1 (7-ounce) can diced green chiles
1 (15.5-ounce) jar salsa
1 pound Cheddar cheese, grated
2 green onions, chopped
1 (2.25-ounce) can sliced black olives

Spread cream cheese in bottom of a round baking dish. Follow with layers of beans, green chiles, and salsa. Top with grated cheese and sprinkle with green onions and olives. Bake at 350° for 15 to 20 minutes. Serve with tortilla chips. Yield: approximately 12 servings.

Green Chile and Cheese Dip

1 (8-ounce) package cream cheese, softened
1 (8-ounce) jar Cheez Whiz
1 (4-ounce) can chopped green chiles
Garlic salt to taste

Combine cream cheese and Cheez Whiz until smooth; add green chiles and garlic salt. Serve with corn chips. Yield: 2 cups.

Santa Fe Soup

1 pound ground beef
1 large onion, chopped
2 (15-ounce) cans pinto beans
1 (15-ounce) can red kidney beans
1 (15.5-ounce) can Rotel diced tomatoes
  and green chiles
1 (14.5-ounce) can cream-style corn
1 (28-ounce) can chopped tomatoes
1 (1-ounce) package taco seasoning mix
1 (0.4-ounce) package buttermilk ranch
  dressing mix

Brown ground beef with onion until done. Drain fat and put beef and onions into a slow cooker. Add undrained beans and vegetables. Stir in taco seasoning mix and dressing mix. Cook on high heat 15 to 20 minutes. Reduce heat, and simmer 4 to 5 hours. Yield: 8 to 10 servings.

Mexican Quiche

1 (10-inch) deep pie shell
6 ounces cooked ham, chopped
3 or 4 slices bacon, fried crisp, crumbled
1 cup shredded Swiss cheese
1 cup shredded sharp Cheddar cheese
2 canned jalapeño peppers, seeded and chopped
1 medium tomato, peeled and chopped
¼ cup chopped onion
3 tablespoons minced fresh parsley
4 eggs, beaten
1 teaspoon dry mustard
½ cup sour cream

In unbaked pastry shell, layer ham, crumbled bacon, Swiss cheese, Cheddar cheese, jalapeño peppers, tomato, onion and parsley. In small bowl, combine beaten eggs, mustard and sour cream. Mix well and pour into pastry shell. Cover edge of pastry with foil to prevent excessive browning. Bake at 450° for 30 minutes or until filling is set. Yield: 6 to 10 servings.

Tortilla Casserole

1 (16-ounce) bag tortilla chips
1 (14.7-ounce) can chili without beans

1 (16-ounce) can refried beans
2 cups grated sharp Cheddar cheese

Alternate layers of half of each ingredient in a 9x13-inch glass casserole dish, beginning with chips, followed by chili, refried beans and cheese. Repeat layers with remaining ingredients. Heat in microwave or oven until cheese melts. Yield: 6 to 10 servings.

Spanish Rice

3 slices bacon
1 cup chopped onion
1 cup raw rice
1 (14.5-ounce) can stewed tomatoes
1 can water
Shredded Cheddar cheese

Sauté bacon until crisp. Cool, crumble and set aside. Sauté onion in bacon grease until tender. Stir in raw rice, stewed tomatoes, water and crumbled bacon. Cook, covered, over low heat 25 minutes. Fluff rice and place in a casserole dish. Cover with shredded cheese. Bake in 350° oven until cheese is melted. Yield: 4 to 6 servings.

Chicken Tortilla

1 (15-ounce) can Rotel tomatoes, mashed
1 (10.75-ounce) can cream of chicken soup
1 (10.75-ounce) can cream of mushroom soup
2 (4-ounce) cans chopped green chiles
Garlic salt to taste
1 onion, chopped
1 clove garlic, minced
2 tablespoons butter
1 package corn tortillas
½ cup chicken broth
3 cups cooked chicken
1 cup shredded Cheddar cheese

Blend tomatoes, soups, green chiles and garlic salt. Sauté onion and garlic in butter; add onion mixture to soup mixture and set aside. Cut corn tortillas cut in fourths and dip in chicken broth. Grease a 9x13-inch casserole pan and layer with tortillas, chicken soup mixture. Repeat layers. Top with grated cheese. Bake in a 350° oven 30 minutes until bubbly. Yield: 8 to 10 servings.

Mexico

Chili and Enchiladas

CHILI CON CARNE:

2 tablespoons salad oil
1 cup chopped onion
3 pounds ground beef chuck
1 (1-pound, 12-ounce) can tomatoes

2 (1.25-ounce) packages chili seasoning
   mix
1 cup red wine
2 (1-pound) cans red kidney beans

Heat oil in large skillet; add onion and sauté until golden; remove to bowl. In same skillet over high heat, cook meat, stirring occasionally, until browned. Stir in sautéed onion, tomatoes, chili seasoning mix, wine and undrained kidney beans. Bring to a boil; reduce heat and simmer, uncovered, 20 minutes or until mixture is slightly thickened. Spoon into a 4-quart, shallow ovenproof serving dish.

ENCHILADAS:

1 dozen corn tortillas
3 cups grated Cheddar cheese
   (¾ pound), divided
1 cup chopped onion

1 (15-ounce) can tomato sauce
2 tablespoons canned chopped green
   chiles

Heat tortillas per package directions. Preheat oven to 350°. In bowl, combine 2 cups grated cheese and onion. Place a rounded tablespoonful of cheese mixture on each tortilla; roll up. Arrange, seam sides down, on chili in baking dish. Combine tomato sauce and chopped green chiles; spoon over tortillas. Sprinkle with remaining 1 cup cheese. Bake 30 to 35 minutes, or until sauce bubbles and cheese melts. Yield: 8 servings.

Mexican Chocolate Sheet Cake

This cake is a huge favorite with family and friends.

CAKE:

2 cups flour

2 cups sugar

½ teaspoon salt

2 teaspoons baking powder

1 tablespoon cinnamon

1 cup water

3 tablespoons cocoa

½ cup shortening

2 eggs

½ cup buttermilk

1 teaspoon baking soda

1 teaspoon vanilla extract

Mix together first 5 ingredients in a large bowl. Place water, cocoa and shortening in a microwave-safe bowl and bring to a boil, stirring after 1 minute. Pour mixture over dry ingredients and mix well. In another bowl, mix eggs, buttermilk, baking soda and vanilla until smooth. Add to the flour mixture. Pour into a greased and floured 9x13-inch pan and bake at 350° for 30 minutes.

CHOCOLATE PECAN FROSTING:

1 stick butter

3 tablespoons cocoa

1 (1-pound) box powdered sugar, sifted

1 teaspoon vanilla extract

1 cup chopped pecans

4 tablespoons milk

While cake bakes, prepare frosting in same microwave-safe bowl used above. Melt butter and cocoa together in microwave oven. Stir in powdered sugar and vanilla until blended. Add pecans. Stir in milk, 1 tablespoon at a time until frosting is of spreading consistency. Frost cake while warm. Yield: 20 servings.

Mexico

German Lenten Dinner

Eva's Kraut Salad

German Hot Potato Salad

Quick Sauerbraten

Brats and Kraut

German Potato Pancakes

Red Cabbage

German Chocolate Cake

Black Forest Cherry Cake

Die Heilige Schrift

Eva's Kraut Salad

1 quart sauerkraut
1 cup chopped celery
1½ cups chopped green bell pepper
2 cans sliced water chestnuts, drained
1 (4-ounce) can chopped pimentos, drained
¼ cup vegetable oil
2 tablespoons water
½ cup vinegar
¾ cup sugar

Mix sauerkraut, celery, bell pepper, water chestnuts and pimentos in a bowl. In a saucepan, add vegetable oil, water, vinegar and sugar. Bring to a boil, stirring occasionally. Pour mixture over vegetables. Refrigerate 24 hours. Yield: 8 to 10 servings.

German Hot Potato Salad

3 pounds potatoes
8 slices bacon
½ cup cider vinegar
1 tablespoon brown sugar
2 teaspoons salt
1 teaspoon celery seed
2 cups chopped celery
½ cup chopped green bell pepper
1 large onion, chopped
2 tablespoons chopped pimentos

Cook potatoes in jackets; peel and dice. Fry bacon crisp; drain and crumble. Mix vinegar, brown sugar, salt and celery seed with ¼ cup bacon grease. Stir in celery, bell pepper, and onion. Heat and pour over hot potatoes. Add chopped pimentos and crumbled bacon. Mix lightly. Yield: 8 servings.

Quick Sauerbraten

1 (4-pound) chuck roast
1 tablespoon vegetable oil
¾ cup chopped onion
3 tablespoons brown sugar
1 teaspoon salt
1 teaspoon coarsely ground pepper
1 teaspoon ground ginger

⅛ teaspoon ground cloves
⅛ teaspoon ground allspice
1 bay leaf
⅔ cup red wine vinegar
1½ cups water, divided
½ cup all-purpose flour

Brown roast on both sides in hot oil in a large Dutch oven. Combine onion, brown sugar, salt, pepper, ginger, cloves, allspice, bay leaf, wine vinegar and 1 cup water; mix well and pour over roast. Cover and simmer 2½ to 3 hours or until roast is tender, turning once. Remove roast to serving platter. Remove bay leaf. Stir remaining ½ cup water into flour; stir into pan drippings. Cook, stirring constantly, until gravy is smooth and thickened. Pour gravy over roast and serve. Yield: 8 servings.

Brats and Kraut

2 tablespoons unsalted butter
1 tablespoon finely chopped onion
1 clove garlic, minced

1 pound fresh bratwurst
1½ cups beer, divided
2 cups sauerkraut

Melt butter in a skillet over medium heat. Add onion and garlic and sauté 4 to 5 minutes. Add bratwurst and ½ cup beer. Cook until beer is evaporated, turning brats often. Add an additional ½ cup beer and continue cooking in the same manner. Add remaining ½ cup beer and continue cooking and turning sausages until the beer has evaporated and sausages are well browned. Transfer bratwurst to a platter. Add sauerkraut to skillet and increase heat to high. Stir 3 to 4 minutes or until hot. Serve with bratwurst. Yield: 6 servings.

Späetzle

2 cups flour
4 eggs
1 teaspoon salt

2 to 3 tablespoons semolina, optional
3 tablespoons water (approximate)

Mix together flour, eggs, salt and semolina (if used). Add water and beat with a spoon or mixer to form a sticky dough until air bubbles appear. Leave to stand 15 to 20 minutes. Meanwhile, bring a pan of salted water to a boil. Fill Späetzle press with dough to within 1¼ inches from the top. Gently squeeze the Späetzle press so that the dough drops into the boiling, salted water. Cook 1 to 2 minutes, stir, and the Späetzle will rise to the surface when done. Scoop from the water with a skimmer. Rinse Späetzle in cold water and place in a sieve to drain off excess water. Transfer to a serving dish and serve. Yield: 6 servings.

German Potato Pancakes

6 large potatoes, cooked and mashed
2 eggs, well beaten
1½ tablespoons flour

¼ teaspoon baking powder
1½ teaspoons salt
1 small onion, grated

Mix together all ingredients in a bowl. Form into 3-inch pancakes and drop into a frying pan with ¼ inch of heated cooking oil. Brown on both sides. Can be served with applesauce. Yield: approximately 1 dozen 3-inch pancakes.

Red Cabbage

2 tablespoons olive oil
1 small onion, chopped
1 clove garlic, minced
½ teaspoon thyme
¼ teaspoon caraway seeds
2 bay leaves
½ teaspoon grated lemon peel
¼ teaspoon pepper
¼ cup plus ½ teaspoon salt, divided
1½ quarts water
1 cup plus 2 tablespoons red wine vinegar, divided
1 small head red cabbage, thinly sliced (about 8 cups)
¼ cup chicken broth

In a large skillet, heat olive oil. Add onion, garlic, thyme, caraway seeds, bay leaves, lemon peel, pepper and ½ teaspoon salt. Cook over medium heat, stirring constantly, until onion is tender. Combine water, 1 cup wine vinegar and remaining ¼ cup salt in a large Dutch oven; bring to a boil. Add cabbage and cook 10 seconds; drain. Add cabbage, remaining 2 tablespoons vinegar and broth to onion mixture; bring to a boil. Cover and reduce heat; simmer 15 to 20 minutes or until cabbage is crisp-tender. Discard bay leaf. Yield: 4 to 6 servings.

German Chocolate Cake

This delicate cake will have a flat, slightly sugary
top crust which tends to crack.

1 (4-ounce) package Baker's German
   sweet baking chocolate
½ cup water
2 cups flour
1 teaspoon baking soda
¼ teaspoon salt

2 sticks butter, softened
2 cups sugar
4 eggs, separated
1 teaspoon vanilla extract
1 cup buttermilk

Heat oven to 350°. Line bottoms of 3 (9-inch) round cake pans with wax paper. Microwave chocolate and water in large microwave bowl on high 1½ to 2 minutes or until chocolate is almost melted, stirring halfway through. Stir until completely melted.

Mix flour, baking soda and salt; set aside. Beat butter and sugar in large bowl with electric mixer on medium speed until light and fluffy. Add egg yolks, 1 at a time, beating well after each addition. Stir in chocolate mixture and vanilla. Add flour mixture alternately with buttermilk, beating after each addition until smooth.

Beat egg whites in another large bowl with electric mixer on high speed until stiff peaks form. Gently stir into batter. Pour into prepared pans. Bake 30 minutes or until cake springs back when lightly touched in center. Immediately run spatula around side of pans. Cool 15 minutes; remove from pans. Remove wax paper. Cool completely on wire racks. Spread Coconut-Pecan Filling and Frosting (recipe below) between layers and over top of cake. Yield: 12 servings.

COCONUT-PECAN FILLING AND FROSTING:

1 (12-ounce) can evaporated milk
1½ cups sugar
1½ sticks butter
4 egg yolks, slightly beaten

1½ teaspoons vanilla extract
1 (7-ounce) package flaked coconut
1½ cups chopped pecans

Combine evaporated milk, sugar, butter, egg yolks and vanilla in large saucepan. Stirring constantly, cook on medium heat 12 minutes or until thickened and golden brown. Stir in coconut and pecans. Cool to room temperature and of spreading consistency. Yield: approximately 4½ cups.

Black Forest Cherry Cake

CAKE:

1 tablespoon butter, softened
6 tablespoons flour, divided
10 tablespoons unsalted butter
6 eggs, at room temperature

1 teaspoon vanilla extract
1 cup sugar
½ cup sifted flour
½ cup unsweetened cocoa

Preheat oven to 350°. Lightly coat the bottoms and sides of 3 (7-inch) round cake pans with softened butter. Sprinkle 2 tablespoons flour into each pan. Tip pans from side to side to spread flour evenly. Remove any excess flour. Set pans aside.

Clarify unsalted butter in a small saucepan by melting it slowly over low heat without letting it brown. Let it rest a minute off the heat and then skim off the foam. Spoon the clear butter into a bowl and set aside. Discard the milky solids at the bottom of the pan.

With an electric mixer, beat eggs, vanilla and sugar together at high speed at least 10 minutes, or until the mixture is thick and fluffy and has almost tripled in bulk.

Combine sifted flour and unsweetened cocoa in a sifter. A little at a time, sift the mixture over the eggs, folding it in gently with a rubber spatula. Finally, add clarified butter, 2 tablespoons at a time. Do not overmix. Gently pour batter into prepared cake pans, dividing it evenly among them.

Bake on middle rack of oven 10 to 15 minutes or until a cake tester inserted into the center comes out clean. Remove from oven and let cool in the pans about 5 minutes. Run a sharp knife around the edges and turn out on racks to cool completely.

KIRSCH SYRUP:

¾ cup sugar
1 cup cold water

⅓ cup Kirsch

Meanwhile, prepare the Kirsch Syrup. Combine sugar and cold water in a small saucepan and bring to a boil over moderate heat, stirring only until sugar dissolves. Boil briskly, uncovered, 5 minutes. Remove from the heat and when the syrup is cooled to lukewarm, stir in the Kirsch.

(continued on next page)

(Black Forest Cherry Cake continued)

Transfer cake layers to a long strip of wax paper and prick each layer lightly in several places with the tines of a long fork. Sprinkle the layers evenly with Kirsch Syrup and let them rest at least 5 minutes.

FILLING AND TOPPING:

3 cups chilled heavy cream
½ cup powdered sugar
¼ cup Kirsch

1 cup poached, pitted, fresh red cherries
(or 1 cup drained and rinsed canned
sour red cherries)

In a large, chilled bowl, beat cream with a whisk or electric beater until it thickens slightly. Sift powdered sugar over the cream and continue beating until firm peaks form on the beater when it is lifted out of the bowl. Pour Kirsch in a thin stream and beat only until the Kirsch is absorbed.

To assemble, place 1 cake layer in center of a serving plate. Spread with a ½-inch-thick layer of whipped cream and strew ½ cup cherries over the top, leaving about ½ inch of the cream free of cherries around the outside. Gently set second layer on top and spread with a ½ inch of whipped cream and remaining ½ cup cherries. Then set third layer in place; spread the top and sides with remaining cream.

To poach fresh cherries: Remove stems and pits, and discard. Combine cherries with 2 cups water and ¾ cup sugar in a small saucepan. Bring to a boil over high heat and then reduce heat to low; simmer 5 minutes or until cherries are tender. Drain in a colander, discarding the syrup, and pat cherries completely dry with paper towels.

CHOCOLATE CURLS:

1 (8-ounce) semisweet chocolate bar or chunk of chocolate, at room temperature

Hold chocolate bar over wax paper or foil, and shave into thin curls with a sharp narrow-bladed vegetable peeler. Draw peeler along the wide surface of the chocolate for large curls, and along the narrow side for small ones. Handle the chocolate as little as possible. Refrigerate or freeze curls until ready for use. Gently press chocolate curls attractively on top. This cake must be refrigerated until serving. Yield: 8 to 10 servings.

Note: May substitute fresh sweet red cherries with stems or maraschino cherries with stems, drained and rinsed, for garnish. Or garnish with both cherries and Chocolate Curls.

Italian Lenten Dinner

Sausage Tortellini Soup

Judith's Antipasto Salad

Tortellini Salad

Spaghetti Bake

Quick Meat Lasagna

Vegetable Lasagna

Asparagus with Orange Sauce

Pasta with Clams

Italian Cream Cake

Sausage Tortellini Soup

1 pound Italian sausage
1 large onion, chopped
1 garlic clove, pressed
3 (14.5-ounce) cans beef broth
2 (14.5-ounce) cans diced tomatoes, undrained
1 (8-ounce) can tomato sauce
1 cup dry red wine

2 carrots, thinly sliced
1 tablespoon sugar
1 teaspoon Italian seasoning
2 small zucchini, sliced
1 (9-ounce) package refrigerated cheese-filled tortellini
½ cup shredded Parmesan cheese

Discard sausage casings. Cook sausage, onion and garlic in a Dutch oven until sausage crumbles and is no longer pink; drain. Stir in broth and next 6 ingredients. Bring to a boil; reduce heat and simmer 30 to 45 minutes. Skim off fat. Stir in zucchini and tortellini; simmer 10 to 15 minutes. Sprinkle each serving with Parmesan. Yield: 10 cups.

Judith's Antipasto Salad

6 ounces spiral macaroni
½ cup olive oil
3 tablespoons red wine vinegar
1 clove garlic, minced
1 teaspoon dried basil
1 teaspoon salt
⅛ teaspoon crushed red pepper flakes
¼ cup grated Parmesan cheese

¾ cup chopped green onions
¾ cup chopped celery
½ cup chopped fresh parsley
2 ounces sliced black olives
8 ounces sliced pepperoni (or cubed Genoa salami)
10 cherry tomatoes, halved
½ cup shredded mozzarella cheese

Cook pasta according to package directions; drain. In a large bowl, stir together oil, wine vinegar, garlic, basil, salt and red pepper flakes. Toss with warm macaroni to coat well. Toss with Parmesan cheese. Cover and refrigerate 2 to 3 hours. Add remaining ingredients, except mozzarella cheese, and toss well. Sprinkle with mozzarella and serve. Yield: 6 servings.

Tortellini Salad

1 (0.6-ounce) package Good Seasons zesty Italian dressing mix, plus
 ingredients to prepare
Fresh tortellini
Genoa salami, chopped in small pieces
Muenster cheese, chopped in small pieces
Fresh parsley, chopped
Cherry tomatoes, halved (optional)
Cooked shrimp (optional)

Prepare dressing mix according to package directions. Set aside. Cook tortellini according to package directions. Add a drop of olive oil to boiling water. This will prevent the tortellini from sticking together, and prevent the dressing from being entirely absorbed. Do not overcook, or tortellini will fall apart when tossed. Drain well.

All other items are used in amounts based on how much tortellini you prepare and the flavor power you want in the final salad. Add ingredients to cooled tortellini. Toss with prepared Italian dressing. Use only enough dressing to lightly coat.

The salad can be prepared the day before and refrigerated. This allows the flavors to develop. This can be served as a side salad or as an entrée served with warm, crusty Italian bread and a glass of wine. Yield: the number of servings is based on the amount of ingredients used.

Note: Fresh tortellini from the cold case at the grocery works best. You can use one or mix the flavors. Flavors include three cheese, chicken herb, or portabella mushroom. (this would depend on where you live and what your local grocery store stocks).

Spaghetti Bake

Olive oil
3 pounds ground beef
2 medium onions, chopped
2 (4-ounce) cans mushrooms
1 (15-ounce) can tomato sauce
1 (12-ounce) can tomato paste
1 teaspoon parsley flakes
2 teaspoons oregano
1 teaspoon basil
1 teaspoon fennel seeds
6 ounces red wine
12 ounces water
1 (16-ounce) package spaghetti
1 (8-ounce) package cream cheese, softened
24 ounces cottage cheese
1 (16-ounce) container sour cream
2 tablespoons chives
Grated Parmesan cheese

Heat oil in a heavy skillet; add ground beef and onion and sauté until meat is browned, stirring to crumble. Drain pan drippings.

Combine mushrooms, tomato sauce, tomato paste, parsley, oregano, basil, fennel seeds, red wine and water. Add to meat mixture, mixing well. Simmer, uncovered, 15 minutes.

Cook spaghetti according to package directions; drain well. Place half the cooked spaghetti in a buttered 9x13-inch baking dish. Combine cream cheese, cottage cheese, sour cream and chives; mix well. Spoon cream cheese mixture over spaghetti layer. Place remaining spaghetti over cream cheese mixture. Pour meat sauce over spaghetti and sprinkle with Parmesan cheese. Bake at 350° for 30 minutes or until bubbly. Yield: 12 servings.

Quick Meat Lasagna

1 pound ground beef
1 (32-ounce) jar spaghetti sauce
1 (16-ounce) container cottage cheese
1 (8-ounce) container sour cream

½ cup grated Parmesan cheese
8 uncooked lasagna noodles
6 ounces sliced mozzarella cheese
1 cup water

Cook meat and drain. Add spaghetti sauce to ground beef and heat. Combine cottage cheese, sour cream and Parmesan cheese. In a 9x13-inch baking dish, layer half the meat sauce, half the noodles, half the sour cream mixture, 4 slices mozzarella cheese. Repeat layers, ending with mozzarella cheese. Pour water around the sides. Cover with foil and bake at 350° for 1 hour. Uncover and bake 20 minutes. Let stand 15 to 20 minutes before serving. Yield: 12 servings.

Vegetable Lasagna

1 (1-pound) box lasagna noodles
2 cups ricotta cheese
¼ cup finely chopped green bell pepper
2 tablespoons finely chopped onion
3 eggs

1 teaspoon dry mustard
Salt and freshly ground pepper to taste
2 cups milk
1 pound mozzarella cheese, sliced or
    thinly shredded

Cook noodles according to package directions. In a small bowl, blend together ricotta cheese, bell pepper and onion. Beat together eggs, mustard, salt and pepper. Stir in the milk. In a shallow 9x13-inch baking dish, arrange half the noodles. Cover with one third of the mozzarella and half ricotta cheese mixture. Place half the remaining mozzarella, and the remaining lasagna noodles over this. Top with ricotta and mozzarella cheeses. Pour milk mixture over all. Place dish in a large pan of hot water, and bake in preheated 350° oven 1¼ hours. Cut lasagna into squares and pass your favorite Italian sauce separately. Yield: 12 servings.

Asparagus with Orange Sauce

1 (9-ounce) package frozen asparagus
1 cup firmly packed brown sugar
2 teaspoons grated orange rind
½ cup fresh orange juice

Cook asparagus according to package directions. Combine brown sugar, orange rind and orange juice in a saucepan, stirring well. Bring to a boil; reduce heat and simmer until thickened (about 5 minutes), stirring often. Serve asparagus with orange sauce. Yield: 1¼ cups.

Pasta with Clams

2 (6.5-ounce) cans minced clams
8 ounces spaghetti, cooked and drained
1 tablespoon butter
1 tablespoon olive oil
1 tablespoon minced garlic
2 teaspoons Italian seasoning
Fresh parsley for garnish

Add clam juice from the cans of clams to boiling, salted water. Place pasta in boiling water and cook according to package directions; drain. In a large skillet, melt butter; add olive oil and garlic. Stir until garlic is light brown in color. Add clams and Italian seasoning; sauté until heated. Add pasta to the clam mixture. Toss together and serve. Garnish with fresh parsley.

Italian Cream Cake

1 stick butter, softened
1 cup vegetable oil
2 cups sugar
5 eggs, separated
1 teaspoon baking soda
1 cup buttermilk
2 cups flour, sifted
1 teaspoon vanilla extract
1 cup shredded coconut
½ cup chopped pecans

Cream butter, oil and sugar; add egg yolks, 1 at a time, beating after each addition. Stir baking soda into buttermilk. Add sifted flour to batter alternating with buttermilk mixture. Stir in vanilla, coconut and chopped nuts. Beat egg whites and fold into mixture. Pour batter into a greased and floured 9x13-inch cake pan for a sheet cake or 3 (8- or 9-inch) layer pans. Bake at 325° for 45 minutes. Cool and ice.

PECAN CREAM CHEESE ICING:

1 (8-ounce) package cream cheese, softened
1 stick butter, softened
1 teaspoon vanilla extract
1 (1-pound) box powdered sugar (3½ cups)
½ cup pecans, chopped fine

Beat cream cheese and butter. Add vanilla, powdered sugar and nuts. Continue to beat until of spreading consistency. Yield: 16 servings for layer cake or 30 bars for 9x13-inch pan.

French Lenten Dinner

Nell's French Onion Soup

Coquilles St. Jacques

Sandy's Crepes à la Florentine

Coq Au Vin

Wendy's Infallible Cheese Soufflé

Beef Bourguignonne

Max's Marinated Mushrooms

Judith's Chantilly Grapes

Betty's Chocolate Éclairs

Joan Ann's Fruit Flan

French foods are always so much fun. Don't be afraid to try the éclairs. They are worth the effort, and I even give you a more simple option if you would like a short cut.

Nell's French Onion Soup

4 large onions, thinly sliced and separated
   into rings
½ cup butter, melted
2¾ cups beef stock (or 2 [10½-ounce] cans
   ready-to-serve beef broth)
2 cups water

¼ cup dry white wine
¼ teaspoon pepper
8 (¾-inch-thick) slices French bread,
   toasted
8 slices Swiss cheese
½ cup grated Parmesan cheese

Sauté onion in butter in a Dutch oven over medium heat 20 minutes or until tender. Gradually add beef stock, water, wine and pepper. Bring to a boil; reduce heat and simmer, uncovered, 15 minutes. Place 8 ovenproof serving bowls on a baking sheet. Place 1 bread slice in each bowl. Ladle soup over bread. Top with 1 cheese slice; sprinkle with Parmesan cheese. Broil 5½ inches from heat until cheese melts. Yield: 8 cups.

Coquilles St. Jacques

2 sliced green onions
¼ cup chopped celery
3 tablespoons butter
1 (4-ounce) can mushrooms, drained
2 tablespoons flour
½ teaspoon salt

¼ teaspoon thyme
⅓ cup white wine
1 pound raw scallops
¼ cup cream
1 egg yolk, beaten

CRUMB MIXTURE:

½ cup breadcrumbs
2 tablespoons melted butter

2 tablespoons Parmesan cheese

Sauté green onions and celery in butter until soft. Add mushrooms. Stir in flour, salt, and thyme. Add wine and cook 12 minutes. Add scallops; heat and stir 5 to 6 minutes. Stir in cream and egg yolk, and cook 3 to 4 minutes more. Divide mixture among 4 scallop shells. Combine Crumb Mixture ingredients and sprinkle over scallop shells. Heat at 350° for 10 to 12 minutes. Yield: 4 servings.

Sandy's Crepes à la Florentine

CREPE BATTER:

4 eggs
¼ teaspoon salt
2 cups flour
2¼ cups milk
¼ cup melted butter
Additional butter for coating pan

Combine eggs and salt. Gradually add flour alternately with milk, beating with an electric mixer or whisk until smooth. Beat in melted butter. Chill at least 1 hour.

FILLING:

2 (10-ounce) packages frozen chopped spinach
½ teaspoon salt
⅛ teaspoon pepper
1 cup ricotta cheese
⅓ cup light cream
3 eggs, beaten slightly
⅛ teaspoon nutmeg
10 to 12 crepes
2 tablespoons melted butter
¼ cup freshly grated Parmesan cheese
¼ cup shredded cheese

Cook spinach according to package directions. Drain and press out liquid. Mix together spinach, salt and pepper. Add ricotta cheese, cream, eggs and nutmeg. Heat a 12-inch nonstick skillet over medium heat. Lightly coat with butter. Add about ⅓ cup batter and swirl to completely cover bottom of skillet. Cook 2 to 3 minutes or until underside is golden brown. Loosen edge of crepe with a rubber spatula then with your fingertips quickly flip the crepe. Cook another minute then remove to plate. Continue until you've used all the batter coating pan with additional butter as needed. Fill crepes with spinach mixture. Roll up and place in a shallow baking dish. Brush with melted butter and sprinkle with combined cheeses. Heat at 350° for 20 minutes or until hot. Yield: 12 servings.

Coq Au Vin

1 (2½-pound) broiler-fryer chicken, quartered
6 slices bacon, diced
2 tablespoons butter
8 whole mushrooms
8 small white onions, peeled
⅔ cup sliced green onion
1 clove garlic, crushed
2½ tablespoons flour

1 teaspoon salt
¼ teaspoon dried thyme leaves
⅛ teaspoon pepper
1½ cups red wine
1 cup canned condensed chicken broth, undiluted
8 small new potatoes, scrubbed
Chopped parsley for garnish

DAY BEFORE SERVING:

Wash chicken and dry with paper towels; set aside. In a Dutch oven, sauté bacon until crisp; remove and drain. Add butter to bacon drippings and heat until melted. Add chicken and brown well all over; remove. Pour off all but 2 tablespoons drippings from Dutch oven.

Add mushrooms and white onions; cook until nicely browned; remove and set aside with chicken. Add green onion and garlic to Dutch oven and sauté 2 minutes; remove from heat. Stir in flour, salt, thyme and pepper. Return to heat and cook, stirring constantly, until flour is browned—about 3 minutes.

Gradually stir in red wine and chicken broth; bring to boiling, stirring. Remove from heat. Stir in bacon, onions and mushrooms; add chicken. Refrigerate, covered, overnight.

SERVING DAY:

Preheat oven to 400°. Add scrubbed potatoes to chicken mixture. Bake, covered, about 1 hour and 50 minutes or until chicken and potatoes are tender. Garnish with parsley. Yield: 4 servings. (Recipe can be doubled easily.)

Wendy's Infallible Cheese Soufflé

LAYERS:

16 slices white bread, crust removed and cut in half
1 pound ham (or Canadian bacon), cut in bite-size pieces
1 pound Cheddar cheese, grated
1 pound Swiss cheese, grated

Arrange in 2 layers in a 9x13-inch pan.

FILLING:

6 eggs, slightly beaten
3 cups milk
½ teaspoon onion salt
½ teaspoon dry mustard

Combine all Filling ingredients and pour over Layers. Cover tightly and refrigerate overnight.

TOPPING:

3 cups crushed corn flakes
½ cup melted butter

Mix cornflakes and melted butter and sprinkle over top. Bake 40 minutes at 375°. Yield: 12 to 16 servings.

Beef Bourguignon

1 stick butter to be used as needed
2½ pounds boneless beef chuck, cut in 1½-inch cubes
3 tablespoons brandy, divided
½ pound (about 12) small white onions, peeled (or substitute canned onions)
½ pound small fresh mushrooms
2½ tablespoons flour
2½ teaspoons meat-extract paste
2 tablespoons tomato paste
1½ cups Burgundy wine
¾ cup dry sherry
¾ cup Ruby port
1 (10.5-ounce) can condensed beef broth, undiluted
⅛ teaspoon pepper
1 bay leaf

In a 4-quart Dutch oven with tight-fitting lid, slowly heat 2 tablespoons butter, but do not burn. In hot butter over high heat, brown beef cubes well in batches, adding more butter as needed. Remove beef as it browns. Return all beef to Dutch oven.

In small saucepan, heat 2 tablespoons brandy just until vapor rises. Ignite; pour over beef. As flame dies, remove beef.

Preheat oven to 350°. Add 2 tablespoons butter to Dutch oven; heat slightly. Add onions; cook over low heat, covered, until slightly brown. Add mushrooms; cook, stirring, 3 minutes. Remove from heat. Stir in flour, meat-extract paste and tomato paste until well blended. Stir in Burgundy, sherry, port and broth. Bring wine mixture just to boiling, stirring. Remove from heat. Add beef, pepper and bay leaf; mix well.

Bake, covered, stirring occasionally, 1½ hours or until beef is tender, adding remaining brandy little by little. Yield: 6 servings.

Max's Marinated Mushrooms

1 pound small fresh mushrooms
4 cups water
1 teaspoon salt
1 (8-ounce) bottle Italian salad dressing
1 large clove garlic, minced
½ teaspoon dried whole thyme

Clean mushrooms and trim stem ends. Combine mushrooms, water and salt in small saucepan. Bring mixture to a boil; cover, reduce heat and simmer 2 minutes. Drain and pat dry. Combine mushrooms with salad dressing, garlic and thyme; cover and refrigerate 8 hours. Mushrooms may be stored in refrigerator 1 week. Yield: 2 cups.

Judith's Chantilly Grapes

2 large bunches green grapes
1 (16-ounce) container sour cream
1 cup light brown sugar
2 teaspoons ground cinnamon
Cointreau liqueur, as desired

Wash grapes; remove stems and chill. When ready to serve, toss grapes in sour cream and place in dessert dishes. Instruct guests to sprinkle desired amount of brown sugar, cinnamon and Cointreau liqueur on their portion. Yield: 12 servings.

Betty's Chocolate Éclairs

Don't be afraid to make these éclairs. They are really easy.

ÉCLAIRS:

½ cup water	½ cup sifted flour
¼ cup butter	2 eggs

Heat oven to 400°. Heat water and butter to rolling boil in saucepan. Stir in flour, stirring vigorously over low heat until mixture forms a ball (about 1 minute). Remove from heat. Beat in eggs, 1 at a time. Beat until smooth. Shape dough with spatula into 6 fingers, each 4 inches long and 1 inch wide. Bake 45 to 50 minutes or until puffed, golden brown and dry. Cool slowly away from drafts.

Cut off tops; scoop out filaments of soft dough. When ready to serve, fill with Vanilla Custard Filling and frost with Thin Chocolate Icing. Yield: 6 éclairs. (Recipe can be doubled.)

VANILLA CUSTARD FILLING:

⅓ cup plus 1 tablespoon sugar	1½ cups milk
¼ cup plus 1 tablespoon flour	2 egg yolks (or 1 whole egg), beaten
Dash salt	1½ teaspoon vanilla extract

Mix sugar, flour, and salt in saucepan. Stir in milk. Cook over medium heat, stirring until it boils. Boil 1 minute. Remove from heat. Stir a little over half of mixture into egg yolks. Blend into hot mixture in saucepan. Bring just to boil. Cool and blend in vanilla.

THIN CHOCOLATE ICING:

½ square (½ ounce) unsweetened chocolate	½ cup powdered sugar
1 teaspoon butter	1 tablespoon boiling water

Melt chocolate and butter over hot water. Remove from heat. Blend in sugar and water. Beat only until smooth but not stiff.

Note: To save time, Éclairs can be filled with prepared French vanilla instant pudding and iced with canned chocolate frosting.

Joan Ann's Fruit Flan

TART PASTRY:

1½ cups flour
½ teaspoon baking powder
½ teaspoon salt

¼ cup cold butter
¼ cup shortening
4 to 6 tablespoons milk

Combine flour, baking powder and salt. Cut in butter and shortening with pastry blender until mixture resembles coarse meal. Sprinkle milk over surface of mixture. Stir with a fork until dry ingredients are moistened. Shape into a ball; chill.

Roll pastry to ⅛-inch thickness on a lightly floured surface. Cut and fit pastry into shallow tart or quiche pan. Bake at 450° for 12 to 15 minutes or until lightly browned.

CUSTARD:

3 egg yolks
¼ cup sugar
2½ tablespoons all-purpose flour

¾ cup milk
3 tablespoons butter
¾ teaspoon vanilla extract

Combine egg yolks, sugar and flour in a medium saucepan, stirring until blended. Stir in milk. Cook over medium heat, stirring constantly, just until mixture comes to a boil. Reduce heat and simmer 1 minute. Cool to lukewarm; add butter and vanilla, stirring until butter melts. Cover and chill thoroughly.

TOPPINGS:

½ cup pineapple preserves

3 cups bite-size fruit*

Cook preserves over low heat until melted. Press preserves through a sieve to remove lumps.

To serve: Spoon Custard into Tart Pastry. Top with fruit as desired. Brush strained preserve liquid lightly over fruit. Yield: 6 servings.

Note: Any type of fresh fruit can be used, but I like to use a combination of blueberries, raspberries, grape halves, sliced peaches, and sliced strawberries.

Oriental Lenten Dinner

Oriental Slaw

Oriental Salad Bowl

Chicken with Cashews

Chicken and Pea Pods

Egg Fried Rice

Confetti Rice

Baked Chop Suey

Chinese Almond Cakes (page 42)

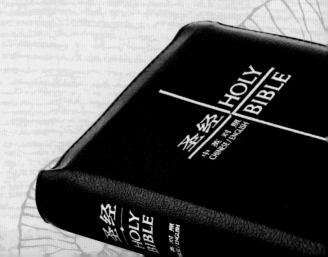

Oriental Slaw

1 (1-pound) package coleslaw
1 bunch green onions, chopped
1 cup sliced almonds
1 (0.9-ounce) package sunflower seeds
  (any nuts may be substituted)

⅔ cup oil
⅓ cup vinegar
½ cup sugar
2 (3-ounce) packages Oriental flavor
  Ramen noodles

Mix coleslaw, onions, almonds and sunflower seeds; set aside. Mix oil, vinegar, sugar and flavor packets from Ramen noodles. Pour mixture over coleslaw and refrigerate several hours. Crush Ramen noodles and add just before serving. Yield: 6 to 8 servings.

Oriental Salad Bowl

3 cups torn fresh spinach leaves
3 cups coarsely chopped Chinese cabbage
½ cup diagonally sliced celery
½ cup coarsely shredded carrots
1 cup bean sprouts
½ cup thinly sliced green onions
35 snow peas, trimmed (about 3 ounces)
1 (8-ounce) can sliced water chestnuts, drained
1 (15-ounce) can miniature corn, drained
¾ cup chow mein noodles
Good Seasons Asian sesame dressing mix, plus ingredients to prepare

Combine spinach, cabbage, celery, carrots, bean sprouts, green onions, snow peas, water chestnuts and corn in a large bowl; toss gently. Garnish salad mixture with chow mein noodles. Serve with Good Seasons Asian sesame dressing, made according to package directions. Yield: 6 servings.

Chicken with Cashews

SEASONING SAUCE:

¼ cup water

¼ cup dry sherry

¼ cup soy sauce

2 tablespoons dark corn syrup

1 tablespoon vinegar

4 teaspoons cornstarch

Combine water, sherry, soy sauce, corn syrup, vinegar, and cornstarch. Blend thoroughly; set aside.

4 large chicken breast halves

¼ cup peanut oil

½ cup chopped green bell pepper

½ cup cashews

2 tablespoons sliced green onions

2 garlic cloves, minced

¼ teaspoon ground ginger

½ teaspoon crushed red pepper

Remove skin from chicken breasts. Cut meat from bone and cut into 1-inch cubes; discard bones. Add oil to wok, pouring it around sides. Heat oil to 325°.

Add chicken cubes; stir-fry 2 to 3 minutes or until chicken turns white. Make a well in center. Add bell pepper and cashews; stir-fry 30 seconds. Make a well in center. Add onions, garlic, ginger, and red pepper; stir-fry 1 minute. Make a well in center.

Stir seasoning sauce and then add to center of wok. Bring to a boil without stirring, about 1 minute. Cook an additional minute or until sauce is thickened, stirring rest of ingredients with the sauce. Yield: 8 to 10 servings.

Note: You may substitute 8 ounces lean pork cut into ½-inch cubes for the chicken.

Chicken and Pea Pods

1½ teaspoons cornstarch
1 tablespoon soy sauce
1 tablespoon dry sherry
1 pound chicken breasts, cut in thin strips
2½ tablespoons oil, divided
1 teaspoon minced garlic
1 teaspoon minced ginger root

½ cup carrot strips
½ cup sliced celery
½ cup sliced green onions
1 (8-ounce) can sliced water chestnuts, drained
1 (9-ounce) package frozen snap peas

Mix together cornstarch, soy sauce and sherry; add chicken. Heat 1 tablespoon oil in a skillet over high heat and stir in garlic and ginger. Add chicken mixture and stir-fry until no longer pink; remove from pan. Add remaining 1½ tablespoons oil and stir-fry carrots and celery 1 minute. Add green onions and stir-fry an additional 30 seconds. Add water chestnuts and pea pods, and stir-fry 30 seconds. Add Sauce to vegetables; cook and stir until bubbles appear. Return chicken to pan to heat through. Yield: 6 servings.

SAUCE:

½ cup chicken broth
2 tablespoons soy sauce

1 tablespoon cornstarch
1 teaspoon sugar

In a small saucepan, mix ingredients over medium heat until warm and blended.

Egg Fried Rice

¼ cup chopped green onions
1 cup frozen green peas
2 tablespoons vegetable oil

3 cups cooked rice
1 egg, slightly beaten
3 tablespoons soy sauce

Sauté green onions and peas in hot oil 2 minutes. Add rice and cook until heated. Push rice mixture to sides of skillet, forming a well in center. Pour egg into well and cook until set, stirring occasionally. Stir rice mixture into egg; add soy sauce, stirring well. Yield: 6 servings.

Confetti Rice

3½ teaspoons vegetable oil, divided
1 egg, beaten
1 carrot, shredded
1 clove garlic, pressed
4 cups cooked rice
1 (20-ounce) can pineapple chunks,
   drained
1 (8-ounce) can water chestnuts, chopped
   and drained
4 ounces cooked ham, julienned
½ cup frozen peas, thawed
⅓ cup chopped green onions
¼ cup soy sauce
¼ teaspoon ground ginger

Heat ½ teaspoon oil in wok or large skillet over low heat. Add egg and swirl around bottom of wok until egg sets in 6-inch pancake; remove and cool. Cut into narrow strips. Heat remaining 3 teaspoons oil in wok over high heat. Stir-fry carrot and garlic about 1 minute or until tender. Add rice, stirring until grains separate. Reduce heat slightly. Stir in pineapple, water chestnuts, ham, peas, onions, soy sauce and ginger; increase heat, and heat through. Gently stir in egg strips. Yield: 6 servings.

Baked Chop Suey

1 pound ground beef
2 medium onions, chopped
1 cup celery, chopped
¼ cup soy sauce
1 (10.75-ounce) can cream of chicken soup
1 (10.75-ounce) can cream of mushroom soup
1 soup can warm water
1 (14-ounce) can Chinese vegetables, drained
Salt and pepper to taste
1 (5-ounce) can chow Mein noodles

Brown ground beef in a skillet and drain. Add remaining ingredients, except Chinese noodles, stirring well to mix. Place in casserole dish and bake uncovered 1 hour at 350°. Cover with noodles. Bake 15 minutes longer. Yield: 4 to 6 servings.

Easter Dinner

Strawberry-Melon Spinach Salad

Stuffed Fresh Ham

Chet's Potatoes

Julie's Vegetable Casserole

Serve With:
Dressing, Gravy and Rolls

Black and White Cream Pie

Piña Colada Cake

I always think of beauty, purity, and color at Easter, which signifies our risen Christ. The salad is a feast of color and really sets the tone. The stuffed ham is a family favorite of the Schmidt family. Wendy got this recipe from her mother. You will need to order a boned fresh ham from your grocer or butcher. This is stuffed and baked with what I call the "rind" or "skin" on. This gets very crisp and can be eaten as well. This is different and a change from the usual Easter ham. You will love this!

Strawberry-Melon Spinach Salad

SALAD:

5 cups bite-size spinach
1 cup sliced fresh strawberries
1 cup honeydew melon balls

⅓ cup broken pecans, toasted
⅓ cup julienne strips Gouda cheese

Toss salad ingredients in a large bowl. Yield: 6 servings.

GINGER-HONEY DRESSING:

2 tablespoons fresh lime juice
2 tablespoons honey

1 tablespoon vegetable oil
¼ teaspoon ground ginger

Shake dressing ingredients in a tightly covered container.

Note: I fix salad plates for this salad, and pass the dressing at the table.

Stuffed Fresh Ham

1 (20-ounce) loaf white bread
2½ sticks butter, divided
1 small onion, chopped
2 celery stalks, chopped
1 tablespoon thyme

Salt and pepper to taste
1 (4-ounce) package slivered almonds
¼ cup milk, more or less
1 fresh ham, ½ pound per serving
**   (see note)**

Toast bread slices and cut into cubes. Melt 2 sticks butter and pour over bread cubes. Sauté onion and celery in remaining ½ stick butter, and mix with bread cubes. Stir in thyme, salt and pepper. Add slivered almonds, and just enough milk to combine. Stuff dressing into ham (see Note) and bake at 350° approximately 30 minutes per pound.

Note: When buying the ham, have a butcher cut out the front bone of the ham so that it forms a pocket. (If he takes all the bones out by mistake, you can always tie one end shut and make your own pocket.)

Chet's Potatoes

1½ pounds potatoes
2 to 4 tablespoons milk
1 (8-ounce) package cream cheese,
  softened
½ cup sour cream

½ cup chopped chives
¼ cup grated Romano cheese
½ teaspoon salt
¼ teaspoon black pepper
Paprika

Cook and mash potatoes. Combine milk, cream cheese, sour cream, chives, Romano cheese, salt and pepper. Add to mashed potatoes. Place in a 1½ quart casserole dish, and sprinkle with paprika. Bake at 350° for 30 minutes. Yield: 6 to 8 servings.

Julie's Vegetable Casserole

½ cup chopped onion
½ cup chopped celery
½ cup chopped green bell pepper
1 (11-ounce) can shoepeg corn
1 (15-ounce) can small peas
4 ounces sour cream

1 (10.75-ounce) can cream of chicken
  soup
1 (2-ounce) jar diced pimentos, drained
½ to 1 cup grated cheese
Townhouse crackers, crushed
⅓ cup butter, melted

Mix all ingredients, except crackers and melted butter in a casserole dish. Sprinkle crushed crackers and melted butter on top. Bake at 350° for 30 minutes. Yield: 8 to 10 servings.

Black and White Cream Pie

CRUMB CRUST:

¾ cup chocolate wafer crumbs
   (about 12 finely crushed)
2 tablespoons grated orange rind

3 tablespoons butter, melted
4 whole chocolate wafers

Put aside about 1 tablespoon each of the wafer crumbs and grated orange rind to garnish the finished pie. Combine remaining crumbs, orange rind and butter. Press firmly and evenly into bottom of buttered 9-inch pie pan with back of a spoon. Cut the whole wafers in half and perch around side of pan, rounded side up. Chill until set, about 45 minutes.

CREAM FILLING:

2⅔ cups milk
1¾ cups sugar
⅓ cup plus 1 tablespoon flour
¼ teaspoon salt
3 small eggs, beaten

1½ tablespoons butter
1¼ teaspoons vanilla extract
1 (1-ounce) square unsweetened chocolate
1 cup heavy cream or (8 ounces Cool
   Whip)

Scald milk in top of double boiler over boiling water. Combine sugar, flour and salt. Gradually stir into milk and cook until thick, stirring constantly. Stir a small amount of the hot mixture into eggs; then quickly pour back in and cook 3 minutes, stirring constantly. Remove from heat. Add butter and vanilla.

To 1 cup of this mixture, add chocolate, and stir until melted and well blended. Pour into chilled Crumb Crust and spread evenly. Carefully pour remaining white cream filling over top to make a second layer. Chill thoroughly for at least 4 hours. Whip the cream and spread over top.

Make a border with reserved cookie crumbs and sprinkle top with reserved grated orange rind. Yield: 6 to 8 servings.

Piña Colada Cake

1 package yellow cake mix*
1 (4-serving-size) package vanilla instant pudding mix
1 (15-ounce) can cream of coconut, divided
½ cup plus 2 tablespoons rum, divided
⅓ cup vegetable oil
4 eggs
1 (8-ounce) can crushed pineapple, drained
**Whipped cream, pineapple chunks, maraschino cherries and toasted
   coconut for garnish**

In a mixing bowl, combine dry cake mix, pudding mix, ½ cup cream of coconut, ½ cup rum, oil and eggs. Beat on medium speed 2 minutes. Stir in pineapple. Pour into well-greased and floured 10-inch Bundt or tube pan. Bake at 350° for 50 to 55 minutes. Cool 10 minutes.

Remove from pan. Poke holes about 1 inch apart in cake. Combine remaining cream of coconut and remaining 2 tablespoons rum; slowly spoon over cake. Chill thoroughly. Top with mounds of whipped cream garnished with pineapple chunks, maraschino cherries and toasted coconut. Store in refrigerator. Makes 1 (10-inch) cake.

Note: Do not use cake mix containing pudding.

Ladies' Spring Luncheon

Sherried Chicken and Grape Salad

Broccoli Salad

Serve With:

Croissants

Orange Sherbet with Mint

My friend Janet has such a flare for presentation! You always know the food will be wonderful and pleasing to the eye. Janet serves this luncheon on china she inherited from her aunt. The luncheon plates are octagonal in shape, trimmed in gold, with a pattern of trees in full spring blossom. She uses the matching teapot as a vase for her flower arrangement in the center of the table.

Sherried Chicken and Grape Salad

6 cups chopped cooked chicken
3 cups sliced black seedless grapes
1 cup toasted slivered almonds
2 celery stalks, diced
3 green onions, minced
1 cup mayonnaise

¼ cup sour cream
4 tablespoons sherry
½ teaspoon seasoned salt
½ teaspoon seasoned pepper
Strawberries, kiwi and mint sprigs for
  garnish

Stir together all ingredients in a large bowl except lettuce. Serve on lettuce leaves. Garnish plate with sliced strawberries, kiwi and mint sprigs. Yield: 6 to 8 servings.

Broccoli Salad

1 cup mayonnaise
2 tablespoons sugar
1 tablespoon red wine vinegar
1 (16-ounce) package fresh broccoli
  florets, chopped

5 bacon slices, cooked and crumbled
1 small red bell pepper, julienned (about
  ½ cup)
½ cup golden raisins
¼ cup finely chopped purple onion

Stir together first 3 ingredients in a large bowl. Add remaining ingredients, tossing well. Yield: 8 to 10 servings.

Orange Sherbet with Mint

Sherbet is served in brandy snifters.
Janet adds a sprig of mint in the sherbet.

Orange Sherbet
Mint sprigs

If you rub your spoon across the mint before diving into the refreshing sherbet, you'll taste a surprising tingle. You simply must try it!

Spring Steak Grill

Cheese Ball with Assorted Crackers

Copper Pennies

Grilled Steak with Whiskey Pepper Sauce

Rice Pilaf

Artichoke and Spinach Casserole

Sweet Beer Bread

Strawberry Tunnel Cream Cake

Before the heat of summer sets in, have a Spring Steak Grill. Decorate the deck, ice down some drinks, beer, and wine, and enjoy these delicious steaks and side dishes. This is an excellent menu for Father's Day and sure to be one of your guests' favorites.

Cheese Ball

4 ounces blue cheese
4 ounces American cheese
1 (5-ounce) jar Old English cheese
6 ounces cream cheese
Onion salt
Garlic powder

Melt all cheeses in microwave on defrost setting until soft. Mix until well blended (may use electric mixer). Chill and then mold into a ball. (This freezes well.) Serve with assorted crackers.

Copper Pennies

2 pounds carrots, sliced crosswise
1 small onion, chopped fine
1 medium green bell pepper, chopped fine
3 ribs celery, chopped fine
1 cup tomato soup, undiluted
1 cup sugar
¼ cup oil
¾ cup apple cider vinegar
1 tablespoon dry mustard
1 tablespoon Worcestershire sauce

Cook sliced carrots in salted water until fork tender; drain. Add chopped onion, bell pepper and celery; set aside. Mix soup, sugar, oil, cider vinegar, dry mustard and Worcestershire in small saucepot; bring to a boil. Pour this hot mixture over the vegetables. Refrigerate overnight. Serve on lettuce. Yield: 10 to 12 servings.

Grilled Steak with Whiskey Pepper Sauce

2 tablespoons chopped white onion
1 tablespoon butter
2 cups beef stock (or canned beef broth), divided
1 clove garlic, pressed
¾ teaspoon cracked black pepper, divided

1 tablespoon whiskey
1 green onion, chopped
2 rib-eyes (or your favorite cut)
1 teaspoon cornstarch
1 tablespoon water

Sauté onion in butter. Add 1 cup stock, garlic and ¼ teaspoon cracked black pepper. Simmer until reduced by half. Add whiskey, green onion and remaining 1 cup stock, and simmer. Sprinkle remaining ½ teaspoon cracked pepper on steak. Place steaks on grill, and sear on both sides. Combine cornstarch and water; add to sauce and heat until thickened. Pour sauce over grilled steaks.

Note: This recipe prepares 2 steaks; increase ingredients as needed for the number of people you will be serving.

Rice Pilaf

2 cups chicken broth
1 cup long grain rice
1 teaspoon Lawry's seasoned salt
½ stick butter
½ cup green onions, chopped

½ cup green bell pepper, chopped
1 (4-ounce) can sliced mushrooms, drained
3 tablespoons diced pimentos

In a medium saucepan, bring broth to boiling, add rice and seasoned salt. Cover tightly, and simmer 20 minutes. Melt butter, sauté onion, bell pepper, and mushrooms. Stir in pimentos, and add mixture to hot rice. Fluff rice with fork, and serve immediately. Yield: 4 servings.

Artichoke and Spinach Casserole

1 (10-ounce) package frozen chopped
  spinach
½ cup chopped onion
4 tablespoons butter
1 cup sour cream
3 eggs, beaten

¼ teaspoon garlic salt
¼ teaspoon black pepper
2 tablespoons lemon juice
¾ cup grated Parmesan cheese
1 (6-ounce) jar artichoke hearts, drained
  and chopped

Cook spinach in a small amount of salted water; drain. Sauté onion in butter; set aside. In a large bowl, combine sour cream, eggs, garlic salt, pepper, lemon juice and half the Parmesan cheese. Combine sautéed onion, drained spinach and artichokes. Add to sour cream mixture. Pour into a greased 2-quart casserole. Sprinkle remaining Parmesan cheese on top. Bake at 350° for 25 to 30 minutes. Yield: 6 servings.

Sweet Beer Bread

The taste of this bread changes with the type of beer
used. The darker the beer, the stronger the flavor.

3 cups self-rising flour
½ cup sugar
1 (12-ounce) bottle beer (non-alcoholic or light beer can be used)
¼ cup butter, melted

Stir together first 3 ingredients; pour into a lightly greased 9 x 5-inch loaf pan and bake at 350° for 45 minutes. Pour melted butter over top and bake an additional 10 minutes.

Cheddar-Chive Beer Bread

Simply add ¾ cup shredded sharp Cheddar cheese and 2 tablespoons chopped fresh chives to dry ingredients and follow above recipe.

Strawberry Tunnel Cream Cake

1 (10-inch) prepared angel food cake
2 (3-ounce) packages cream cheese, softened
1 (14-ounce) can sweetened condensed milk
⅓ cup lemon juice from concentrate
1 teaspoon almond extract
2 to 4 drops red food coloring, optional
1 cup chopped fresh strawberries, plus whole berries for garnish
1 (12-ounce) carton whipped topping, divided

Invert cake onto serving plate. Cut a 1-inch slice crosswise from top of cake; set aside. With sharp knife, cut around cake 1 inch from center hole and 1 inch from outer edge, leaving cake walls 1 inch thick. Tear cake from center, leaving 1-inch-thick base on bottom of cake. Reserve torn cake pieces.

In a large mixing bowl, beat cream cheese until fluffy. Gradually beat in sweetened condensed milk until smooth. Stir in lemon juice, almond extract and food coloring. Stir in reserved torn cake pieces and chopped strawberries. Fold in 1 cup whipped topping. Fill cavity of cake with strawberry mixture; replace top slice of cake. Chill 3 hours or until set. Frost with remaining whipped topping. Garnish with fresh strawberries, if desired. Store in refrigerator. Yield: 16 servings.

Memorial Day Steak Supper

Oyster Spread

Fruited Cheese Spread

Grilled Corn on the Cob in the Husk

Dill and Roquefort Green Bean Salad

Swiss Scalloped Potatoes

Italian Rib-Eyes

Lemonade Poke Cake

Oyster Spread

2 (8-ounce) packages cream cheese,
   softened
¼ cup milk (or evaporated milk)
2 to 3 tablespoons mayonnaise
1 tablespoon lemon juice
1 tablespoon Worcestershire sauce

Dash hot sauce
Salt to taste
2 (3⅔-ounce) cans smoked oysters,
   minced
Paprika
Chopped parsley

Combine cream cheese, milk, mayonnaise, lemon juice, Worcestershire, hot sauce and salt; blend well. Stir in oysters and refrigerate several hours. Sprinkle with paprika and parsley before serving. Yield: about 3 cups.

Note: Recipe can be halved.

Fruited Cheese Spread

Prepare the first layer only of the Show-Stopping Torte in the New Year's Eve Celebration menu (page 62). It is great on crackers.

Grilled Corn on the Cob in the Husk

Corn on the cob with husks
Butter, softened
Spices or herbs of choice

Remove large outer husks from corn. Turn back inner husks and remove silk. Mix butter with any spice or herb of choice. Spread butter mixture over corn. Pull husks back over ears and tie with fine wire. Place corn on grill 3 inches from medium coals; cover and cook 15 to 20 minutes, turning frequently, until corn is tender.

Dill and Roquefort Green Bean Salad

DILL DRESSING:

1 cup Wesson oil
¼ cup white vinegar
3 tablespoons lemon juice
½ teaspoon cracked black pepper
¼ teaspoon paprika
½ teaspoon dry mustard

1 or 2 garlic cloves
1 tablespoon dill seed
¼ pound Roquefort or blue cheese, crumbled
¼ cup mayonnaise
2 tablespoons sour cream

SALAD:

2 pounds fresh green beans (or 2 [1-pound] cans)
Ham hock
1 onion, chopped
Lawry's seasoned salt

Salt and pepper to taste
1 garlic clove, minced
½ pound bacon
1 bunch green onions, chopped

DAY BEFORE SERVING:

Put all Dill Dressing ingredients in a jar and shake well. Refrigerate. Yield: 1½ cups.

Cook the beans with ham hock, onion, seasoned salt, salt, and pepper in a small amount of water. When tender, drain and cool. This is important for a well-flavored salad. Refrigerate until the next day.

SERVING DAY:

Fry bacon until crisp; drain, and crumble. Mix the drained green beans with green onions and half the crumbled bacon; toss with the Dill Dressing. Chill several hours. Garnish with the remaining half of the bacon when ready to serve. Yield: 6 to 8 servings.

Note: This can easily be doubled. If you are serving a big crowd, 30 or more, double the amounts in the Dill Dressing. This is delicious served with barbecue or charcoaled meats.

Swiss Scalloped Potatoes

1½ cups shredded Swiss cheese, divided
½ cup sliced green onions including tops
1 tablespoon dill weed
2 tablespoons butter
2 tablespoons flour
1 teaspoon salt
1 cup milk
1 cup sour cream
6 to 7 cups cooked, peeled, thinly sliced potatoes (about 4 large)
¼ cup fine dry breadcrumbs
¼ cup butter, melted

In a small bowl, toss together 1cup Swiss cheese, green onions and dill weed; set aside. In a 1-quart saucepan, melt butter; stir in flour and salt. Gradually stir in milk. Cook over medium heat, stirring constantly until thickened. Cook 2 additional minutes. Remove from heat and stir in sour cream.

In a shallow, 3-quart buttered baking dish, layer one third of potatoes, one half of the Swiss cheese mixture, and one half of sour cream mixture. Repeat layers, topping with last third of the potatoes. Combine breadcrumbs, melted butter and remaining ½ cup Swiss cheese. Sprinkle over top of casserole. Bake in preheated oven at 350° for 30 to 35 minutes. Yield: 8 to 10 servings.

Note: Three cups diced ham can be included in layering to make this a meat-vegetable dish. These are fantastic!

Italian Rib-Eyes

1 green bell pepper, chopped	¼ teaspoon salt
1 bunch green onions, cut into 1-inch pieces	¼ teaspoon pepper
	¼ cup olive oil
3 garlic cloves, minced	2 tablespoons butter, melted
2 cups sliced fresh mushrooms	4 (1¼-inch-thick) rib-eye steaks
2 tablespoons dried Italian seasoning	1 large tomato, chopped

Sauté first 7 ingredients in hot oil and butter in a large skillet over medium-high heat until tender. Cover vegetable mixture and keep warm. Grill steaks, covered with grill lid, over high heat (400° to 500°) about 16 minutes for medium, or to desired degree of doneness, turning occasionally. Stir tomato into vegetable mixture; spoon over steaks. Yield: 4 servings.

Note: This is also very good using grilled chicken breast instead of steaks.

Lemonade Poke Cake

1 package lemon cake mix, plus ingredients to prepare
1 (6-ounce) can frozen lemonade concentrate, thawed
¾ cup powdered sugar
1(12-ounce) tub soft-whipped fluffy white (or fluffy lemon ready-to-spread) frosting

Heat oven to 350°. Prepare and bake cake as directed on package for 9x13-inch rectangular pan. Cool 15 minutes. Stir together lemonade concentrate and powdered sugar. Poke warm cake with a fork at ½-inch intervals, wiping fork occasionally to reduce sticking. Drizzle lemonade mixture evenly over cake. Refrigerate cake until cold. Spread cold cake with frosting. Cover and refrigerate any leftover cake.

Mexican Fiesta

Serve With:
Tub of Margaritas

Chili Con Queso

Rotel Cheese Dip

Mexican Two-Bean Salad

Gazpacho

Tangy Taco Ring

King Ranch Cheesy Casserole

Mexican Banana Pudding

We Southerners have a real passion for our neighbors in Mexico. We love Mexican food, the laid back atmosphere, and the vibrant, happy colors. Bring your sombreros and Mexican blankets and enjoy your own Mexican Fiesta. One of the great things about Mexican food is that each dish feeds many. Each of these dishes can be made a day ahead so you, as the hostess, can enjoy the fiesta with your guests.

Chili Con Queso

2 slices bacon
3 green onions, chopped
2 pounds Velveeta cheese, cubed
¼ cup milk
2 (4-ounce) cans chopped green chiles
1 (10-ounce) can Rotel tomatoes and green chiles
Garlic powder to taste
Pinch chili powder (or cayenne pepper)

Fry bacon crisp; drain and crumble. Sauté onions in bacon drippings. Add cheese and melt over low heat. After cheese melts, add milk, stirring constantly until incorporated. Add remaining ingredients and stir to blend flavors. Heat over low heat about 10 to 15 minutes. If too thick, just add more milk. Serve hot with chips.

Rotel Cheese Dip

1 pound Velveeta cheese
1 (10-ounce) can Rotel tomatoes and green chiles

Cut cheese into cubes, and place in a microwave-safe dish. Melt on high 2 minutes. Stir in Rotel tomatoes and green chiles. Serve hot or cold with a chip assortment.

VARIATIONS:

1. Add a (15-ounce) can hot tamales, chopped.

2. Add ½ pound ground beef, cooked with onions and garlic.

Mexican Two-Bean Salad

1 (15-ounce) can great Northern beans, rinsed and drained

1 (15-ounce) can black beans, rinsed and drained

4 plum tomatoes, chopped

½ teaspoon black pepper

6 green onions, chopped

½ cup salsa

¼ cup red wine vinegar

2 tablespoons chopped fresh cilantro

½ teaspoon salt

1 medium green bell pepper, chopped

Combine all ingredients; serve immediately or cover and chill. Toss gently before serving. Yield: 6 servings.

Gazpacho

1 (14-ounce) can diced tomatoes

1 (13-ounce) can chicken broth

1 medium cucumber, chopped

½ cup sliced green onion

¼ cup red wine vinegar

¼ teaspoon liquid hot sauce

Mix all ingredients together in a large bowl. Refrigerate 2 to 3 hours before serving. Yield: 4 servings.

Tangy Taco Ring

½ pound ground beef, browned
1 (1.25-ounce) package taco seasoning
1 cup shredded Cheddar cheese

2 tablespoons water
2 (8-ounce) tubes crescent rolls
Salsa and sour cream, optional

Combine ground beef, taco seasoning, Cheddar cheese and water together in a mixing bowl; set aside. Divide crescent rolls into triangles. Arrange triangles in a circle on a baking sheet with the bases overlapping and the pointed ends toward the outside. Push dough edges together until you have a solid 5-inch circle. Spoon meat mixture into the center of rolls; fold points of triangles up over the filling and toward the center, pinching dough together where the points meet. Bake at 350° until golden brown, about 20 to 25 minutes. Serve with salsa and sour cream for topping, if desired. Yield: 4 to 6 servings.

King Ranch Cheesy Casserole

2 (7.25-ounce) boxes Kraft macaroni and
    cheese, plus ingredients to prepare
1 (10- to 12-count) package flour tortillas
1 (10-ounce) can Rotel tomatoes with
    green chiles
1 medium onion, chopped

1 cup chicken broth
1 (10.75-ounce) can cream of mushroom
    soup
1 (10.75-ounce) can cream of chicken
    soup
1 cup shredded Cheddar cheese

Prepare macaroni and cheese according to package directions. Layer tortillas in a 9x13-inch casserole dish coated with cooking spray. Layer prepared macaroni and cheese mixture on top of tortillas. Mix remaining ingredients, except Cheddar cheese. Pour over macaroni and cover with shredded Cheddar cheese. Refrigerate 8 hours. Bake at 350° for 45 minutes. May be frozen. Yield: 10 to 12 servings.

Tres Banana Pudding

1 (14-ounce) can sweetened condensed milk
1 1/2 cups cold milk
1 (16-ounce) carton heavy cream
1 (4-serving) package vanilla instant pudding mix
36 vanilla wafers
3 medium ripe bananas
Cinnamon for topping (optional)

Place a mixing bowl in the refrigerator. In a separate large bowl, combine sweetened condensed milk and milk. Add pudding mix, and beat well. Place in refrigerator and remove chilled mixing bowl. Add heavy cream to mixing bowl and beat with electric mixer until stiff peaks form. Fold into pudding mixture. Spoon 1 cup pudding mixture into a large, glass serving bowl and top with a third of the wafers. Slice bananas into 1/4-inch-thick rounds; place a third of sliced bananas over wafers in bowl. Repeat layering twice, beginning and ending with pudding. Cover with a light dusting of cinnamon. Chill before serving. Refrigerate leftovers. Yield: 12 servings.

Note: This is beautiful made in a trifle bowl or a glass salad bowl. The mixture can also be layered in individual serving dishes.

Mexican Stack Party

Easy Salsa

Guacamole

Black Bean Salsa

Taco Soup

Key Lime Pie
Easy Ice Box Key Lime Pie

What would we do without Mexican food? It is so easy to prepare and feeds many. In this menu, you can either make the salsa and guacamole from scratch with the recipes provided, or you can buy them already prepared. Either way works.

Don't let the word "soup" in Taco Soup bother you. This dish has the consistency of chili. This must be served over regular-size Frito corn chips, and then the fun begins with adding the toppings. This dish does not freeze well. The ingredients do not retain their identity. The recipe can be doubled and prepared in a large Dutch oven.

Easy Salsa

1 (14.5-ounce) can Mexican-style stewed tomatoes
1 (10-ounce) can Rotel tomatoes and green chiles
1 (4½-ounce) can chopped green chiles
½ cup chopped fresh cilantro
2 tablespoons dried minced onion
1 teaspoon ground cumin
1 teaspoon garlic salt
½ teaspoon garlic powder
Tortilla chips

Combine first 3 ingredients in a food processor or blender. Add cilantro, onion, cumin, garlic salt and garlic powder and blend well. Place in an airtight container and chill at least 4 hours before serving with tortilla chips. Yield: 1½ cups.

Guacamole

3 ripe avocados
½ cup chopped tomato
¼ cup finely chopped onion
1 chopped jalapeño pepper, optional
1 tablespoon lemon or lime juice
1 teaspoon salt
Freshly ground black pepper
Hot sauce or salsa to taste, optional

Cut each avocado in half and scoop out pulp. Save 1 seed to place in the serving bowl to prevent browning. Mash and add all remaining ingredients. Stir until well blended. Serve with tortilla chips.

Black Bean Salsa

3 medium tomatoes, seeded and chopped
1 (15-ounce) can black beans, rinsed and
   drained
¾ cup fresh or frozen corn
½ cup finely chopped red onion
½ cup chopped roasted sweet red pepper
1 jalapeño pepper, finely chopped
2 tablespoons minced fresh cilantro

¼ cup lime juice
1 garlic clove, minced
1 teaspoon dried oregano
1 teaspoon ground cumin
½ teaspoon salt
½ teaspoon ground coriander
Tortilla chips

In a large bowl, combine all ingredients except tortilla chips. Cover and refrigerate for at least
2 hours before serving. Serve with tortilla chips. Yield: 4 cups.

Taco Soup

2 pounds ground beef
1 onion, chopped
1 (15-ounce) can pinto beans
1 (15-ounce) can Ranch-style beans
1 (15-ounce) can whole-kernel corn
1 (4.5-ounce) can chopped green chiles
1½ (10-ounce) cans Rotel tomatoes and green chiles
1 (1-ounce) envelope ranch dressing mix
1 (1-ounce) package taco seasoning
Fritos, regular size
Shredded cheese, chopped lettuce, chopped tomatoes, chopped black olives, sour
   cream and sliced jalapeño

Brown ground beef and chopped onion; drain off fat. Add beans, corn, green chiles, tomatoes,
ranch dressing mix and taco seasoning. Cook until heated through. Serve over Fritos. Garnish
with cheese, lettuce, tomatoes, olives, sour cream and jalapeños. Yield: 8 to 12 servings.

Key Lime Pie

CRUST:

1¾ cups graham cracker crumbs
2 tablespoons sugar

6 tablespoons butter, melted

Combine all Crust ingredients; press onto bottom and 1 inch up sides of a 9-inch springform pan. Cover and chill at least 1 hour.

FILLING:

3 large eggs, separated
1 (14-ounce) can sweetened condensed
  milk
½ cup fresh Key lime juice

1 tablespoon lemon juice
2 teaspoons grated Key lime rind
2 tablespoons sugar

Whisk egg yolks; add condensed milk, juices and rind, whisking until smooth. Beat egg whites at high speed with an electric mixture until foamy; gradually add sugar, beating until soft peaks form. Fold into yolk mixture; spoon into prepared Crust.

Bake at 325° for 15 to 20 minutes or until set and lightly browned. Cool on a wire rack; cover and chill 8 hours.

TOPPING:

1 cup whipping cream
1 tablespoon powdered sugar
½ teaspoon vanilla extract

Quartered lime slices for garnish,
  optional

Beat whipping cream at high speed with electric mixer until slightly thickened; add powdered sugar and vanilla, beating until soft peaks form. Remove sides of springform pan and dollop whipped cream around top of pie. Garnish with quartered lime slices, if desired. Yield: 8 slices of pie.

Key Lime Pie

Easy Icebox Key Lime Pie

1 (14-ounce) can sweetened condensed milk
½ cup lime juice
1 teaspoon grated lime rind, optional
2 egg yolks
1 (8-inch) crumb crust

In medium-size bowl, combine milk, juice and rind. Stir in egg yolks and pour into crust. This can be topped with Cool Whip or whipped cream.

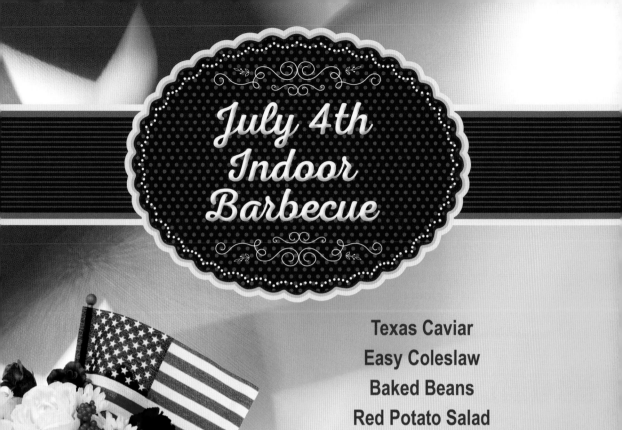

July 4th Indoor Barbecue

Texas Caviar

Easy Coleslaw

Baked Beans

Red Potato Salad

Best Ever Smoked Barbeque Brisket

Serve With:
Dinner Rolls

Lemon Icebox Cheesecake

If you're like I am and work for a living, then you need something simple for this holiday. I love to have family and friends over before the traditional Fourth of July fireworks display at Little Rock's Riverfront Park. It needs to be easy but good, and what's a good Fourth of July without barbeque? I make the potato salad, slaw, and cheesecake the night before. The flavors in the slaw and potato salad need to blend overnight anyway. I also mix up the baked beans, and they're ready for the oven.

All I have to do the next day is pop the brisket in the oven and, when it's almost done, pop the beans in the oven. I enjoy family and friends with no hassle of preparing food!

Texas Caviar

2 (15.8-ounce) cans black-eyed peas, drained
1 (14.5-ounce) can petite diced tomatoes, drained
2 fresh jalapeños, stemmed, seeded and minced
1 small onion, diced
½ yellow bell pepper, stemmed, seeded and diced
¼ cup chopped fresh cilantro
6 tablespoons red wine vinegar
6 tablespoons olive oil (not extra virgin)
½ teaspoon salt
½ teaspoon black pepper
½ teaspoon garlic powder
1 teaspoon dried oregano
1½ teaspoons ground cumin

Mix all ingredients in a medium bowl; cover and refrigerate 2 hours or up to 2 days. The longer it sits, the better the flavor. Before serving, adjust seasonings if desired. Transfer to a serving bowl and serve with chips of choice.

Easy Coleslaw

1 (16-ounce) package shredded coleslaw (found in salad section)
1 tablespoon seasoned salt
1 tablespoon sugar
1 tablespoon vinegar
1 cup Miracle Whip salad dressing

Empty packaged coleslaw into a large bowl. Add next 3 ingredients and mix well. Stir in salad dressing and mix well. (Water can be added for a thinner dressing.) Chill at least 4 hours before serving. Yield: 4 to 6 servings.

Baked Beans

1 (22-ounce) can pork and beans
¼ cup chopped onion
¼ cup cola
¼ cup brown sugar
¼ cup tomato ketchup
¼ teaspoon salt
4 dashes Worcestershire sauce
4 dashes Tabasco sauce
Cooked bacon or sausage, optional

Combine all ingredients in a large saucepan and simmer on top of stove 45 minutes, or bake at 350° approximately 1 hour. Yield: 4 to 6 servings.

Red Potato Salad

5 pounds red potatoes
½ teaspoon salt
Black pepper to taste
1 green or red bell pepper, chopped
1½ cups chopped celery
1 onion, chopped
1½ cups sweet pickle relish
1 (6-ounce) can pimentos, chopped
6 hard-boiled eggs, sliced
1 tablespoons mustard
1½ cups Miracle Whip salad dressing

Boil potatoes in water with salt until done. Test by piercing with a fork. Cube cooled potatoes. Mix remaining ingredients together and add to cooled potatoes. Refrigerate overnight for best flavor. Yield: 8 to 10 servings.

Note: If you live in a household like I do, where raw onion is not appreciated, you can substitute onion salt to taste.

Best Ever Smoked Barbeque Brisket

1 (8- to 12-pound) whole brisket
1 (4-ounce) bottle liquid smoke
Garlic salt
Celery salt
1 large onion, sliced
½ (15-ounce) bottle Lea & Perrins Worcestershire sauce (do not substitute any other brand)
1 (18-ounce) bottle Kraft Original BBQ sauce

Trim almost all fat from brisket. (You need to leave some fat for flavor and moisture.) After trimming, place brisket in baking pan and pour liquid smoke over top. Liberally season with garlic salt and celery salt, and cover surface with onion slices. Cover and refrigerate overnight. Before cooking, discard onion slices. Pour off liquid smoke and douse with Worcestershire sauce. Cover with heavy-duty foil and bake in a 275° oven 5 hours. Uncover and pour barbeque sauce over the top. Bake, uncovered, 1 hour. Slice meat thinly and serve with sauce. Store leftover meat in the refrigerator in the remaining sauce. After cooling, remove any fat off the top of the sauce. Leftovers will keep for several days in the refrigerator. Yield: allow ½-pound per person.

SERVING SUGGESTIONS:

You can make open-faced sandwiches on sandwich buns. Add coleslaw on top of the brisket for a traditional barbeque sandwich.

Shredded beef salad: place shredded beef atop your favorite salad greens and serve with your favorite dressing.

Create a new menu with a salad, potato, vegetable and dessert.

This is a very versatile dish—good for a crowd. I've used this recipe for over 20 years, and it is one of the most consistent recipes I've ever tried. Always good!

Lemon Icebox Cheesecake

1 (3-ounce) package lemon Jell-O
1 cup boiling water
1 (12-ounce) can Carnation evaporated milk, chilled
1 (14-ounce) box cinnamon graham crackers, divided
2 cups sugar, divided
1 stick butter, melted
1 (8-ounce) package cream cheese, softened
¼ cup lemon juice

Mix Jell-O and boiling water. Stir till dissolved and chill.

Note: If the mixture does not gel, it doesn't matter. When you beat it into the cream cheese mixture, it will dissolve.

Whip evaporated milk until the consistency of whipped cream.

Place 2 sleeves from the box of graham crackers in a food processor, and process into 2 cups crumbs. Reserve 1 cup crumbs for topping. Mix remaining 1 cup crumbs with 1 cup of sugar, then stir in melted butter. Press mixture into bottom of a 9x13-inch pan. Place in refrigerator.

Beat cream cheese, remaining 1 cup sugar and lemon juice. Mix with prepared Jell-O and beat until smooth. Fold in whipped evaporated milk. Spread on top of chilled crust. Top with reserved cinnamon graham crumbs. Chill and serve. Yield: 12 servings.

Hawaiian Pool Party

Mai Tai Compote

Calypso Broccoli Salad

Hawaiian Chicken Salad

Salsa Shrimp in Papaya

Barb's Chicken Balinese

Aunt Hallie's Hawaiian
Wedding Cake

Mai Tai Compote

1 medium fresh pineapple	1 cup halved strawberries
1 orange, peeled and sliced	½ cup seedless red grapes
1 kiwifruit, peeled and sliced	1 firm banana

Cut pineapple in half lengthwise through crown. Remove fruit with curved knife, leaving shells intact (cover and refrigerate shells until ready to serve). Trim off core and cut fruit into chunks. In large bowl, combine pineapple, orange, kiwi, strawberries and grapes. Banana will be sliced and added just before serving.

DRESSING:

¼ cup fresh lime juice	1 tablespoon orange-flavored liqueur
3 tablespoons honey	½ teaspoon grated lime peel
1 tablespoon light rum	

Combine Dressing ingredients. Pour over fruit. Toss gently to coat and refrigerate, covered, 1 hour. Just before serving, slice banana into fruit salad. Toss gently and spoon salad into reserved pineapple shells to serve. Yield: 6 to 8 servings.

Calypso Broccoli Salad

2 cups broccoli pieces	2 cups coarsely chopped green cabbage
1 cup sliced fresh mushrooms	½ cup cubed Cheddar cheese
½ cup prepared creamy buttermilk salad dressing	½ cup cubed Swiss cheese
	2 tomatoes, chopped

Partially cook broccoli by plunging into rapidly boiling water 2 minutes, or microwave on high 2 minutes; drain. In a large bowl, combine broccoli and mushrooms with dressing. Toss gently to coat. Cover and refrigerate at least 2 hours to blend flavors. Before serving, toss broccoli mixture with cabbage, cheeses and tomatoes. Yield: 5 to 6 servings.

Note: I like to substitute ½ head cauliflower, chopped, for the tomatoes.

Hawaiian Chicken Salad

This salad can be served cold, unbaked, as well as hot.

4 cups chopped cooked chicken
1 (8-ounce) can crushed pineapple in natural juice, drained
1 small apple, chopped
1 celery stalk, chopped
1 small onion, chopped
½ cup chopped green bell pepper
1 cup mayonnaise
¼ teaspoon salt
¼ teaspoon ground ginger
2 cups Honey Almond Delight brand cereal, crushed to 1 cup
1 tablespoon butter, melted

To serve hot: preheat oven 350°. In 1½-quart baking dish, combine chicken, pineapple, apple, celery, onion and bell pepper. In small bowl, combine mayonnaise, salt and ginger. Add to chicken mixture, stirring until well combined. In separate small bowl, combine cereal and butter. Sprinkle evenly over chicken mixture and bake 25 to 30 minutes until hot. Yield: 6 servings.

Salsa Shrimp in Papaya

Lemon juice to taste
12 ounces shelled bay shrimp, cooked, rinsed and drained
¾ cup chunky salsa of choice
½ teaspoon Lawry's lemon pepper seasoning
¼ teaspoon Lawry's garlic powder with parsley
3 ripe papayas, halved, peeled and seeds removed
Lettuce leaves
Fresh chopped parsley and lemon slices for garnish

In medium bowl, sprinkle lemon juice over shrimp. Add salsa, lemon pepper and garlic powder; cover and marinate in refrigerator 1 hour or overnight. Fill each papaya half with marinated shrimp. Arrange papaya halves on lettuce leaves. Garnish each with chopped parsley and lemon slices. Yield: 6 servings

Barb's Chicken Balinese

2 (6-ounce) boxes wild rice mix, prepared according to package directions
2 (3-ounce) cans chow mein noodles
4 whole chicken breasts, marinated in teriyaki sauce overnight, sliced and stir-fried
4 (10.5-ounce) cans Franco American chicken gravy, heated, divided
Chopped tomatoes
Sliced almonds
Chopped green onions
Chopped celery
1 (20-ounce) can crushed pineapple, drained
Grated Cheddar cheese
Shredded coconut

Place each ingredient in separate bowls, arranging them in order given. Divide gravy into two bowls, with second bowl between grated cheese and coconut. Guests prepare their plate by layering each ingredient, starting with rice and ending with coconut. This is a lot of fun for all. Yield: 6 servings.

Aunt Hallie's Hawaiian Wedding Cake

CAKE:

1 box Duncan Hines white cake mix, plus ingredients to prepare

Prepare cake mix according to package directions. Pour into a 9x13-inch pan and bake at 350° for 26 to 33 minutes. Cool.

FROSTING:

2 cups milk
1 (6-ounce) package vanilla instant pudding mix
1 (8-ounce) package cream cheese, softened
1 (20-ounce) can crushed pineapple, drained dry
1 (9-ounce) container Cool Whip
1 (3.5-ounce) can Angel Flake coconut

Mix milk and pudding together in a large bowl. Add creamed cheese and mix well. Add pineapple to pudding mixture. Spread over cake. Top with Cool Whip and coconut. Yield: 12 servings.

Seafood Buffet

Boiled Shrimp Ring

Shrimp Gumbo

Barbecue Shrimp

Crawfish Étouffée

Beer-Battered Fried Shrimp

Piña Colada Shrimp

Crusty Fried Oysters

Oven-Fried Potato Wedges

Beer-Battered Hush Puppies

Oyster Rockefeller Casserole

Bread Pudding with Fruit and Whiskey Sauce

This is a real seafood lover's menu. If you insist on including appetizers, buy a can or two of smoked oysters and pre-prepared boiled shrimp ring from your local grocer. Open the oyster, drain and rinse. Serve all with crackers and cocktail sauce.

Shrimp Gumbo

3 pounds peeled shrimp
2 quarts water
1 tablespoon McCormick seafood
  seasoning
3 tablespoons salad oil
3 tablespoons flour

1 medium onion, chopped
½ bell pepper, chopped
6 green onions, chopped
2 stalks celery, chopped
1 (14.5-ounce) can diced tomatoes,
  drained

Boil shrimp, until pink in color, in water with McCormick seafood seasoning. Remove shrimp when cooked and save the water. Do not overcook the shrimp. In a large saucepan, make a roux by mixing salad oil and flour; brown to a dark brown color, stirring constantly. Add onion, bell pepper, green onions and celery to the roux. Cook until vegetables are wilted. Add roux and vegetables to the shrimp water. Add tomatoes and stir. Return shrimp to mixture 5 minutes before serving. Serve over fluffy rice.

Barbecue Shrimp

4 pounds unpeeled, large fresh shrimp
2 lemons, cut into wedges
2 bay leaves
1 cup butter, melted
1 cup ketchup
½ cup Worcestershire sauce

4 garlic cloves, chopped
3 tablespoons Old Bay seasoning
1 teaspoon dried rosemary
1 teaspoon dried thyme
French bread

Place shrimp in a 9x13-inch pan and top with lemon wedges and bay leaves (use a disposable pan to make cleanup easy). Stir butter and next 6 ingredients together. Pour over shrimp. Bake at 400° for 35 minutes or until shrimp are pink, stirring every 10 minutes. Discard bay leaves and serve with bread and lemon wedges. I like to peel the shrimp and leave the tails intact. Depending on the size of the shrimp, they will cook quicker than 35 minutes. When they are pink, they are done. Do not overcook. Yield: 6 to 8 servings.

Crawfish Étouffée

2 pounds crawfish tails with fat
2 teaspoons hot sauce
½ teaspoon ground red pepper, divided
¼ cup vegetable oil
¼ cup all-purpose flour
2 celery stalks, chopped
2 large onions, chopped
2 large green bell peppers, chopped
½ cup chopped green onions
¼ cup water
½ teaspoon salt
¼ teaspoon ground black pepper
¼ cup chopped fresh parsley
4 cups hot cooked rice

Remove package of fat from crawfish tails and set aside. Sprinkle crawfish with hot sauce and ¼ teaspoon red pepper.

Combine oil and flour in a 4-quart Dutch oven; cook over medium heat, stirring constantly, until roux is the color of chocolate (10 to 15 minutes).

Stir in celery and next 3 ingredients; cook until vegetables are tender, stirring often. Add crawfish tails and water; cook, uncovered, over low heat 15 minutes, stirring occasionally. Stir in 2 tablespoons crawfish fat (reserve remaining fat for other uses), salt, black pepper, and remaining red pepper; simmer 5 minutes. Stir in parsley. Serve over rice. Yield: 6 servings.

Beer-Battered Fried Shrimp

2 pounds large unpeeled shrimp
½ cup all-purpose flour
½ cup cornstarch
½ teaspoon salt
½ cup beer

¼ cup butter, melted
2 egg yolks
Vegetable oil
Bottled cocktail sauce

Peel shrimp, leaving tails intact; devein, if desired. Combine flour, cornstarch and salt. Add beer, butter and egg yolks; stir until smooth.

Pour oil to a depth of 2 inches into a Dutch oven; heat oil to 375°. Dip shrimp into batter; fry, a few at a time, until golden brown. Drain. Serve with cocktail sauce. Yield: 6 servings.

Piña Colada Shrimp

Once on vacation to Marco Island, Florida, we bought everything we needed to make Piña Coladas and found that our condo had no blender. So I decided to try the Piña Colada mix (instead of an egg) to dip the shrimp in before coating them with the cornmeal mix. You've heard of coconut shrimp—well these are even better! It has become one of our favorites!

2 pounds large shrimp, peeled and butterflied
½ cup piña colada bottled mix
2 cups self-rising cornmeal mix
Vegetable oil

Dip each shrimp in piña colada mix and then coat with cornmeal. Place on a plate and refrigerate 30 minutes. This allows the shrimp to dry so the coating stays on the shrimp during cooking. (This same method of allowing the coating, whether meal or flour, to dry in the refrigerator before frying can be used with any other breaded item.)

Pour oil to a depth of 2 inches into a Dutch oven. Heat oil to 400° and cook shrimp until golden brown. Drain on paper towels to remove excess oil. Yield: 6 servings.

Crusty Fried Oysters

1 large egg, beaten
2 tablespoons cold water
1 (12-ounce) container fresh select oysters, drained
1½ cups saltine cracker crumbs
Vegetable oil

Combine egg and water. Dip oysters in egg mixture and roll each in cracker crumbs. Deep-fry in 375° oil, a few at a time, about 2 minutes or until golden brown, turning to brown both sides. Drain on paper towels. Yield: 3 servings.

Oven-Fried Potato Wedges

2 large baking potatoes (1½ pounds)
1½ tablespoons olive oil
1 teaspoon garlic salt
1 teaspoon seasoned pepper
1 teaspoon dried onion flakes
1 teaspoon dried Italian seasoning

Cut potatoes into ½-inch-wide strips. Combine potatoes and olive oil in a large heavy-duty, zipclose plastic bag and shake to coat.

Combine garlic salt, seasoned pepper, onion flakes and Italian seasoning; add to potatoes and shake until evenly coated.

Spread potatoes in a 10x15-inch jelly-roll pan coated with cooking spray. Bake at 450° for 25 to 28 minutes or until done, stirring after 15 minutes. Yield: 4 servings.

Beer-Battered Hush Puppies

Beer adds zip to this hush puppy batter. For a more traditional
hush puppy, leave out the bell pepper and tomato.

1½ cups self-rising yellow cornmeal
¼ cup self-rising flour
2 small onions, finely chopped
1 medium-size green bell pepper, finely
 chopped
1 tomato, finely chopped

1 large egg, lightly beaten
1½ teaspoons Worcestershire sauce
Dash hot sauce
½ cup beer
Vegetable oil

Combine cornmeal and flour in a large bowl; stir well. Add onion, pepper and tomato. Stir in
egg, Worcestershire and hot sauce. Add beer, stirring well. Pour oil to a depth of 2 inches into
a small Dutch oven; heat oil to 375°. Carefully drop batter by rounded tablespoonfuls into
hot oil; fry hush puppies, a few at a time, 1 to 2 minutes or until golden brown, turning once.
Drain on paper towels. Yield: 3½ dozen.

Oyster Rockefeller Casserole

1 stick butter
1 rib celery, finely chopped
1 medium onion, finely chopped
1 (10-ounce) box frozen chopped spinach,
 thawed and drained
½ cup chopped parsley

¼ teaspoon anise seed
¼ cup Lea & Perrins Worcestershire sauce
½ cup breadcrumbs, plus more to top
Salt, pepper, and cayenne to taste
1 quart raw oysters, drained
1 cup shredded sharp Cheddar cheese

Melt butter in a medium saucepan and sauté celery. Add onions spinach, parsley, anise seed,
Lea & Perrins, ½ cup breadcrumbs, salt, pepper and cayenne. Grease a shallow casserole
dish and arrange oysters in a single layer. Cover with Rockefeller (spinach) mixture. Bake
at 450° for 30 minutes. Remove and sprinkle with shredded cheese and a very thin layer of
breadcrumbs. Bake an additional 10 minutes until slightly brown. Yield: 4 to 6 servings.

Bread Pudding with Fruit and Whiskey Sauce

½ (1½-pound) loaf of bread, torn in pieces
2½ cups milk
4 eggs, beaten
6 tablespoons butter, melted
3 tablespoons packed brown sugar
1 cup sugar
1½ teaspoons vanilla extract
½ teaspoon almond extract
1 (16-ounce) can sliced apples, peaches or fruit cocktail, undrained
1½ teaspoon ground nutmeg

Preheat oven to 350°. Mix bread and milk in a large mixing bowl; set aside until milk is absorbed. With mixer set on low speed, beat in eggs and butter. Stir in sugars, extracts and fruit. Pour batter into a 9x13-inch pan that has been coated with vegetable spray. Sprinkle top with nutmeg. Bake 30 to 35 minutes until top is browned. Yield: 10 servings.

WHISKEY SAUCE:

1 stick butter
2 cups powdered sugar

¼ cup water
2 tablespoons bourbon

Combine butter, powdered sugar and water in a small saucepan; mix well. Cook over medium heat until sugar dissolves. Reduce heat to medium low and continue cooking 3 minutes or until mixture starts to thicken. Remove from heat and stir in bourbon. Pour over warm bread pudding.

Note: Sauce can be reheated over low heat, but do not allow to boil. If it thickens too much, add water, 1 teaspoon at a time, and heat until it reaches the desired consistency.

Labor Day Weekend Dinner

Easy Appetizer:
Gouda Round and Crackers

Cranberry-Walnut Green Salad

Fried Rice

Garlic Butter Snow Peas

Teriyaki Pork Loin

Grilled Pork Tenderloin with Jezebel Sauce

Strawberry Cream Layered Dessert

We've enjoyed the summer, the kids are back in school, and entertaining moves in out of the heat. This Strawberry Cream Layered Dessert makes summer linger a little longer. Let's talk over summer vacations one last time and then turn our thoughts to fall and all it has to offer. Football will be the talk, particularly in the South.

Cranberry-Walnut Green Salad

CARAMELIZED WALNUTS:

¾ cup walnuts
Olive oil

Sugar

Heat walnuts in a small amount of olive oil in a skillet. Remove from pan and roll in enough sugar to coat. Return to skillet and heat until sugar is melted while stirring frequently to prevent scorching. Cool before adding to salad. Walnuts may be stored in refrigerator up to 2 weeks.

SALAD:

1 (size) packet Good Seasons Italian
  dressing mix
Olive oil
Rice vinegar (no substitutions)

3 ounces crumbled blue cheese
¾ cup dried cranberries
¾ cup caramelized walnuts
1 (8-ounce) package spring mix greens

Make dressing according to package directions. Combine salad ingredients in salad bowl and toss to coat with dressing. Yield: 4 to 6 servings.

Fried Rice

3 strips bacon, diced
¾ cup chopped green onions and tops
⅓ cup diced red bell pepper
¼ cup frozen green peas, thawed

1 egg, beaten
4 cups cold, cooked rice
2 tablespoons soy sauce

Cook bacon in wok or large skillet over medium heat until crisp. Add green onions, bell pepper and peas; stir-fry 1 minute. Add egg and scramble. Stir in rice and cook until heated, gently separating grains. Add soy sauce; cook and stir until heated through. Serve immediately. Yield: 6 to 8 servings.

Garlic Butter Snow Peas

1 tablespoon butter
1 clove garlic, minced
½ teaspoon seasoned salt
1 (8-ounce) package frozen snow peas
1 tablespoon extra-virgin olive oil
1 teaspoon fresh lemon juice
Salt and pepper to taste

Melt butter in a skillet over medium heat. Add garlic and cook, stirring constantly, about 1 minute. Stir in Italian seasoning and snow peas; mix well and cook just until peas are warmed through. (Don't overcook.) Stir in olive oil and lemon juice. Season with salt and black pepper. Serve immediately.

Teriyaki Pork Loin

I am giving you two pork recipes to choose from. You can choose to cook indoors with the Teriyaki Pork Loin or take advantage of outdoor grilling season one last time with Grilled Pork Tenderloin with Jezebel Sauce (on following page).

1 (3-pound) boneless pork loin roast
1 cup teriyaki sauce
3 tablespoons brown sugar
3 tablespoons dry sherry
1 teaspoon minced fresh gingerroot

1 garlic clove, minced
¼ cup water
2 tablespoons sugar
1 tablespoon cornstarch

Pierce meaty parts of roast with a large fork; place in large zipclose bag. Combine teriyaki sauce, brown sugar, sherry, ginger and garlic; pour over roast. Press air out of bag; close securely. Refrigerate 8 hours or overnight, turning bag over occasionally. Put roast and marinade in a Dutch oven and cook at 350° about 1 hour to 106 to 165° on thermometer. Remove roast from oven; let stand 10 minutes before slicing. Meanwhile, add water, sugar and cornstarch to the marinade in the Dutch oven. Cook over medium heat until thickened, stirring occasionally. Serve teriyaki glaze with roast. Yield: 6 to 8 servings.

Grilled Pork Tenderloin with Jezebel Sauce

MARINADE:

1½ cups olive oil
¾ cup soy sauce
½ cup red wine vinegar
⅓ cup fresh lemon juice
¼ cup Worcestershire sauce
6 sprigs parsley, leaves only, chopped

2 tablespoons dry mustard
1 tablespoon black pepper (freshly cracked if possible)
2 cloves garlic, peeled and minced
4 (1-pound) pork tenderloins

Combine oil, soy sauce, wine vinegar, lemon juice, Worcestershire, parsley, mustard, pepper and garlic in medium glass or ceramic baking dish. Add pork and turn to coat in the marinade. Cover and marinate in refrigerator, turning meat occasionally 8 to 10 hours or overnight. Preheat grill to 350°. Drain pork, discarding marinade, and pat dry. Put pork on grill, cover with lid, and grill, turning occasionally until meat thermometer reads 160°, approximately 15 to 20 minutes. Let stand 5 minutes before carving.

JEZEBEL SAUCE:

3 tablespoons prepared horseradish, drained
3 tablespoons dry mustard
¾ cup pineapple preserves

¾ cup apple jelly
1 tablespoon coarsely ground black pepper
Fresh rosemary for garnish

Combine horseradish and mustard in a medium saucepan. Whisk in preserves, jelly and ground pepper; heat until jelly melts. Transfer to a serving bowl and set aside.

Arrange pork on serving platter and garnish with branches of fresh rosemary. Serve Jezebel Sauce on the side.

Strawberry Cream Layered Dessert

FIRST LAYER:

½ cup flour
½ cup butter

½ cup nuts

Combine flour, butter and nuts. Press into a 9x13-inch baking dish, and bake at 350° for 10 minutes or until very light brown. Cool.

SECOND LAYER:

1 (8-ounce) package cream cheese, softened

1 cup powdered sugar
1 cup frozen non-dairy whipped topping

Beat cream cheese, powdered sugar and whipped topping together. Spread over cooled First Layer.

THIRD LAYER:

2 pounds fresh strawberries, hulled and sliced
1 cup sugar
1 cup water
⅛ teaspoon salt
3 tablespoons cornstarch
1 (3-ounce) box strawberry Jell-O
1 (16-ounce) container frozen non-dairy whipped topping
Whole fresh strawberries for garnish

Spread sliced strawberries on top of Second Layer. Mix sugar and water together. Stir in salt and cornstarch, and cook until thickened. Add strawberry Jell-O; stir well and cool. Pour cooled mixture over berries and top with whipped topping. Garnish with whole fresh strawberries. Yield: 12 servings.

Authentic German Oktoberfest

Heisser Deutscher Kartoffelsalat (Hot German Potato Salad)

Krautsalat (Sweet-Sour Coleslaw)

Bratwurst in Beer

Kartoffelpuffer (Potato Pancakes)

Gefüller Kohl or Kohlrouladen (Stuffed Cabbage or Rolled Cabbage)

Rot kohl and Apfel (Red Cabbage and Apples)

Black Forest Cream Pie

Apfelukuchen (Fresh Apple Cake)

My daughter Lyndsey's godparents, Jan and Bob Grant, are both of German heritage. These recipes are a combination from both sides of the family. This is a great menu preceded by a cheese round, assorted crackers, and a relish tray of dill pickles, pickled okra, cauliflower, and mini corn on the cob. Bring out the beer steins, put on the German music, and begin the party. Don't forget, you'll need a designated driver tonight.

Heisser Deutscher Kartoffelsalat
(Hot German Potato Salad)

8 medium red potatoes	2 teaspoons all-purpose flour
2 celery stalks, chopped	½ teaspoon salt or to taste
½ green bell pepper, chopped	¼ teaspoon ground black pepper
1 hard-boiled egg, grated	¾ cup beer, divided
½ cup chopped fresh parsley	4 tablespoons cider vinegar or to taste
6 slices bacon, chopped	1 tablespoon plus 1 teaspoon sugar
½ medium onion, chopped	1 tablespoon deli-style brown mustard

Cook potatoes in a large pot of boiling salted water over high heat 15 to 20 minutes until tender. Drain and rinse potatoes in cold water. Set aside to cool.

Mix celery, bell pepper, egg and parsley in a large bowl. Slice potatoes fairly thick and add to celery mixture.

Fry bacon in a pan until crisp. Remove bacon to paper towel, reserving drippings in pan. Add onion to bacon drippings and cook until soft. Stir in flour, salt and pepper. Pour in ½ cup beer, vinegar, sugar and mustard. Stir, and bring to a boil. Reduce heat and simmer 2 or 3 minutes.

Pour sauce over potato mixture and toss to combine. Finished dish should be moist but not runny. Adjust consistency with remaining beer as needed. Add chopped bacon; stir. Serve warm. Best if made on the day of the meal. Yield: 8 to 10 servings.

Krautsalat (Sweet-Sour Coleslaw)

1 large head cabbage, shredded
1 medium onion, chopped
1 green bell pepper, finely chopped
1 tablespoon salt
1 cup boiling water
1 cup sugar

½ cup vegetable oil
1 cup white vinegar
1 tablespoon celery seed
1 teaspoon mustard seed
1 (2-ounce) jar diced pimentos

Mix cabbage, onion and bell pepper in large bowl. Sprinkle with salt and pour boiling water over mixture. Cover and let stand at room temperature 1 hour. Drain.

Combine sugar, oil, vinegar, celery seed and mustard seed. Add to cabbage mixture. Stir in diced pimentos. Cover and refrigerate at least 2 hours. This can be kept for several days in the refrigerator. Yield: 8 servings.

Bratwurst in Beer

Heavy-duty aluminum foil pan
1 (12-ounce) can beer, or more as needed
1 (19-ounce) package your favorite Brats
1 (12-ounce) package Brat rolls
Condiments of choice, such as mustard, sauerkraut, grilled onions, etc.

Prepare grill heat source (charcoal or gas) in usual manner. Place foil pan on direct heat position on grill and fill with beer. Prick bratwurst on all sides with a fork and place in beer pan to parboil several minutes. Relocate pan to indirect heat position on grill. Remove brats from pan and place on grill over direct heat. Grill 5 to 8 minutes, turning occasionally, until lightly browned. Transfer brats back to pan of beer. Cover pan with foil. Cook an additional 30 minutes or until done. Serve with rolls and condiments of choice. Yield: 6 to 8 servings, depending on quantity of Brats.

Kartoffelpuffer (Potato Pancakes)

8 medium potatoes (about 3 pounds)
1 medium to large onion
1 egg, beaten
3 tablespoons all-purpose flour

1 teaspoon salt
¼ teaspoon ground black pepper
Dash garlic powder
½ cup vegetable oil

Peel potatoes and place in cold water to prevent discoloring. Using a hand grater, shred potatoes and onion. Using a strainer, press out as much juice as possible, saving the juice. Once juice has settled, pour away the liquid on top and reserve about ¼ cup of the starchy sediment on the bottom. Return the ¼ cup of starchy sediment to the potato-onion mixture. Add egg, flour, salt, pepper and garlic powder to mixture; stir.

In a large 12-inch skillet, heat oil (about ¾-inch deep) over medium-high heat. Scoop up a level ¼ cup of potato mixture and drop into skillet. With oiled spatula, flatten into cake about ¼-inch thick. Fry in batches, about 4 at a time. Brown pancakes until crisp, 2 to 3 minutes per side. Remove and drain on paper towels. May be topped with applesauce, sour cream or granulated sugar, to taste. Yield: 12 to 16 servings.

Gefüller Kohl or Kohlrouladen
(Stuffed Cabbage or Rolled Cabbage)

THE DAY BEFORE:

1 pound ground chuck

1 pound ground pork

3 small eggs, beaten

1 tablespoon butter

2 medium yellow onions, chopped

1 teaspoon garlic and pepper seasoning

1 teaspoon salt

1 (10.75-ounce) can condensed tomato
  soup

½ (5-ounce) canister unseasoned
  breadcrumbs

2 tablespoons Worcestershire sauce

Place ground chuck and pork into a large mixing bowl; add eggs. Melt butter in a large skillet over medium heat. Add onion and sauté until soft and slightly brown. Add cooked onion, garlic and pepper seasoning, salt and tomato soup to meat mixture. Alternately knead breadcrumbs and Worcestershire into meat mixture until stiff enough to form a soft ball. Cover bowl with plastic wrap and refrigerate overnight.

THE DAY OF SERVING:

1 large head green cabbage

2 (15-ounce) cans diced tomatoes

2 (15-ounce) cans Bavarian-style
  sauerkraut

Cut core from cabbage. Remove and discard wilted or decayed outer leaves. In a large pot, bring enough salted water to a boil to cover the cabbage head. Immerse cabbage into boiling water. Cook over medium-high heat 5 to 10 minutes or until leaves become tender and separate from head. Gently remove leaves as they become tender. Drain on paper towels to cool. Trim any large stems. Spread a cabbage leaf flat, inner side up. Place 2 or 3 teaspoons of meat filling near base of leaf. Fold bottom of leaf over filling; then fold sides toward center. Roll tightly. Repeat with remaining filling and cabbage leaves. Secure with toothpicks as necessary on smaller leaves.

Combine tomatoes and sauerkraut and spread half on the bottom of a large roasting pan. Add a layer of stuffed cabbage leaves loosely, side by side, on the mixture. Add a second layer of stuffed cabbage leaves and cover with remaining tomato-sauerkraut mixture. Preheat oven to 325°. Cover pan and bake about 3 hours or until meat is done. Yield: 8 to 12 servings. Leftovers freeze well in plastic containers.

Rotkohl und Apfel (Red Cabbage and Apples)

3 tablespoons butter
1 large onion, chopped
1 small to medium head red cabbage, shredded
3 firm Granny Smith apples, peeled, cored and shredded
¾ cup water
½ cup red wine
3 tablespoons apple cider vinegar
2 teaspoons sugar
1 teaspoon salt
½ teaspoon ground nutmeg
¼ teaspoon ground black pepper
1-2 tablespoons fresh lemon juice

Melt butter in a large pot over medium heat. Add onion and sauté about 10 minutes until tender. Add cabbage and apples. Cook another 10 minutes, stirring occasionally. Add water, wine, cider vinegar, sugar, salt, nutmeg and pepper; stir. Cover pot and simmer over low heat until cabbage is tender, about 30 to 40 minutes. Check occasionally. If cabbage gets dry, add a small amount of hot water. When cabbage is tender, remove from heat. Stir in lemon juice to taste. Serve warm. (May be prepared a day in advance and gently reheated.) Yield: approximately 8 servings.

Black Forest Cream Pie

CRUST:
1 (9-inch) frozen pastry crust (or crumb crust)

If using frozen pastry crust, bake following package directions, and cool.

FILLING:
6 ounces semisweet chocolate chips
2 tablespoons butter
1 (8-ounce) package cream cheese, softened
¼ cup powdered sugar
1 (21-ounce) can cherry pie filling, divided

(continued on next page)

(*Black Forest Cream Pie continued*)

Melt chocolate and butter in microwave on defrost cycle 30 seconds or until melted; stir to blend. In small bowl, beat cream cheese and powdered sugar until blended and then add chocolate mixture. Beat until smooth. Fold in 1 cup cherry pie filling. Set aside remaining cherry pie filling. Spread mixture into pie shell and chill 1 hour in refrigerator.

TOPPING:

1 cup whipping cream (or frozen whipped topping)
Semisweet chocolate chips for garnish

Whip cream or use defrosted frozen whipped topping and spread over chilled pie. Spread reserved pie filling over whipped topping in a band around the outer edge of the pie and garnish the center with chocolate chips. Yield: 12 servings.

Apfelukuchen (Fresh Apple Cake)

2 eggs
2 cups sugar
1½ cups oil
1 teaspoon vanilla extract
½ cup applesauce
3 cups sifted all-purpose flour

¼ teaspoon salt
1 teaspoon baking soda
1 teaspoon baking powder
1 teaspoon cinnamon
1 teaspoon grated nutmeg
2½ cups finely chopped cooking apples

Heat oven to 300°. Grease and flour a Bundt pan. In a large mixing bowl, beat together eggs, sugar, oil and vanilla. Add applesauce. Sift together flour, salt, baking soda, baking powder, cinnamon and nutmeg. Add to the sugar and egg mixture and beat until well blended. Stir in apples. Bake at 300° about 1½ hours. Pour Glaze over warm cake.

GLAZE:

½ cup apple juice
1½ cups powdered sugar

Grated rind and juice of 1 lemon

In a saucepan, heat apple juice and add powdered sugar, lemon juice and grated lemon rind. Beat until smooth. Pour over warm cake.

Halloween Dinner

Party Meatballs

Cranberry Salad

Steamed Broccoli with Lemon-Butter Sauce

Wild and Cheesy Chicken

Pear Cobbler

Party Meatballs

1 (10-ounce) jar grape jelly, melted
1 (12-ounce) bottle chili sauce
Prepared frozen meatballs

Combine jelly and chili sauce in a slow cooker. Add frozen meatballs and heat thoroughly. Serve with toothpicks.

Cranberry Salad

1 (12-ounce) package fresh cranberries
1 (20-ounce) can crushed pineapple, drained
⅔ cup sugar
1 cup chopped pecans
½ pint whipping cream, whipped (or Cool Whip)

Grind cranberries in food chopper or food processor. Stir in drained pineapple and sugar. Refrigerate overnight. Add pecans and whipped cream mix and refrigerate several hours before serving. Yield: 8 servings.

Steamed Broccoli with Lemon-Butter Sauce

1 bunch fresh broccoli (or frozen broccoli spears)
1 stick salted butter, melted
Lemon juice to taste

Trim ends of fresh broccoli and cut into stalks. Steam in a saucepan or pressure cooker. (If using frozen broccoli, follow package directions.) Add lemon juice to melted butter and pour over steamed broccoli. Yield: 4 servings.

Wild and Cheesy Chicken

1 medium whole chicken
1 (6-ounce) box Uncle Ben's long grain and wild rice
3 tablespoons butter
1 small onion, chopped
½ cup chopped celery
1 cup sliced fresh mushrooms
1 (10.75-ounce) can cream of chicken soup
1½ cups grated longhorn cheese
1 package slivered almonds, toasted

Boil fryer in water to cover until done. Remove from broth, reserving broth. Debone when cool and dice.

Cook rice according to package directions, using reserved broth for liquid. Melt butter in medium saucepan; add onion, celery and mushrooms. Sauté gently until tender. Mix with chicken, rice and soup and pour into greased 9x13-inch casserole. Top with grated cheese and toasted almonds. Bake at 350° for 30 minutes. Yield: 6 to 8 servings.

Pear Cobbler

FRUIT MIXTURE:

2 cups sugar

1 teaspoon vanilla extract

1 stick butter, cut in small chunks

3 cups sliced pears (about 6 pears)

2 heaping tablespoons flour

1 cup water

1 teaspoon nutmeg

Mix sugar, vanilla and butter and stir together with pears. Mix flour with water and pour over pears, mixing well. Place mixture in a deep casserole dish and sprinkle nutmeg over top.

DOUGH:

1½ cups flour

⅔ cup shortening

¼ teaspoon baking powder

2 or 3 tablespoons water

Mix flour, shortening, baking powder and water together, mixing well. Dough will be thinner than regular pie dough. Divide dough in half. Roll out one half of dough to ¼-inch thickness on floured board and cut into strips. Bake strips on a cookie sheet in a 425° oven until golden brown. Submerge strips in pear mixture.

Roll out remaining dough and place over top of cobbler. Use a knife to make slashes in top crust to allow steam to escape. Bake at 425° about 1 hour or until crust is browned. Serve warm cobbler with vanilla ice cream. Yield: 6 to 8 servings.

Thanksgiving Dinner

Orange Fluff Salad
Turkey
Brown Gravy
Green Beans Almondine
Mashed Potatoes
Cornbread Dressing
Corn Pudding
Spinach Casserole
Sweet Potato Casserole
Serve With:
Rolls
Layered Pumpkin Pie
Pecan-Cranberry Pie
Lemon Curd Pound Cake
Bacardi Rum Cake

There is something here for everyone, including traditional turkey, dressing, gravy, and sweet potatoes. Be sure to put the Spinach Casserole, Sweet Potato Casserole, and Corn Pudding in casserole dishes. This makes it easy to go from refrigerator, oven, and back to the refrigerator for storage.

Orange Fluff Salad

1 (6-ounce) box orange Jell-O
1 (8-ounce) carton small curd cottage cheese
1 (20-ounce) can crushed pineapple, drained
1 (15-ounce) can mandarin oranges, drained
1 (8-ounce) carton frozen whipped topping

Stir all ingredients together except whipped topping. Fold in topping. Refrigerate overnight. Serve on a lettuce leaf. Yield: 12 servings.

Foil-Wrapped Baked Turkey

Defrost turkey in refrigerator 3 days. Remove giblets and neck. Wash bird and pat dry. Place bird in the middle of a large piece of heavy-duty foil, and wrap by bringing ends to meet over the bird and rolling down. Tuck in sides. Place in refrigerator until ready to place in pan and roast. Roast at 450° to an internal temperature of 185°.

7 to 9 pounds	2¼ to 2½ hours
10 to 13 pounds	2¾ to 3 hours
14 to 17 pounds	3½ to 4 hours
18 to 21 pounds	4½ to 5 hours
22 to 24 pounds	5½ to 6 hours

Other Turkey Preparation Methods

DEEP-FRIED TURKEY:

1 (10-pound) turkey, thawed and completely dried with paper towels
Salt, pepper and garlic powder to taste
2 tablespoons dry rub to taste
Your favorite marinade for injecting
3 to 5 gallons peanut oil

Make sure to remove giblets from turkey. Season with salt, pepper and garlic powder and your favorite dry rub. Inject marinade in the thick areas. When injecting, slowly pull the needle as you are pushing the plunger to prevent the marinade from pooling in one area. This more evenly distributes the marinade. Let the turkey come to room temperature before frying.

To fry, follow turkey fryer directions and safety precautions. The turkey cannot be left unattended during the frying time. Keep children away from the fryer at all times.

SMOKED BRINED TURKEY:

2 cups kosher salt
2 cups packed brown sugar
½ cup soy sauce

½ cup Worcestershire sauce
1 (10-pound) turkey
¼ cup extra virgin oil

For the brine, place 2 cups water, salt, brown sugar, soy sauce, Worcestershire and any additional spices of choice, such as rosemary, ginger or onion, in a pot and bring to a boil, stirring well. Cool.

Mix cooled brine with 2 gallons ice water, and pour over turkey in non-scented white kitchen garbage bag placed in a roasting pan. Tie the bag and turn several times, coating the turkey. After 6 hours, turn the bag to brine other side for 6 additional hours. Do not brine the turkey more than 12 hours.

Remove turkey from brine and rinse very well inside and outside. Pat dry and baste with oil. Preheat smoker to 225°. Place turkey on middle rack of smoker, and smoke 5 to 6 hours (30 to 35 minutes per pound). or until the internal temperature reaches 165°. Cover wings and drumsticks halfway through smoking, and place foil over breast once it reaches 150°. Let the turkey rest 15 minutes before carving.

Brown Gravy

¼ cup flour
½ cup water
1 (14-ounce) can chicken broth

1 bouillon cube
Kitchen Bouquet

Stir flour and water until smooth. In a saucepan, heat chicken broth and bouillon cube until bouillon cube is dissolved. Slowly add flour mixture; stir until gravy is thickened. Add Kitchen Bouquet until desired color is reached. Yield: 1¾ cup.

Green Beans Almondine

1 (16-ounce) bag frozen green beans
¾ cup water
1 teaspoon salt

1 tablespoon rendered bacon grease
1 tablespoon butter
1 small package slivered almonds

Place green beans in a pressure cooker with water, salt and bacon grease. Cook 3 minutes. Remove from heat. Melt butter in a small frying pan. Stir in almonds; cook till golden brown. Place green beans in a serving dish and sprinkle almonds on top. Yield: 6 to 8 servings.

Mashed Potatoes

6 medium potatoes
1 stick butter
Milk

Green onions, paprika or parsley for
  garnish

Peel and slice potatoes. Place in pressure cooker and cook 4 minutes. Drain water and mash potatoes with butter. Add milk until desired consistency is reached. Garnish with green onions, paprika or parsley. Yield: 6 to 8 servings.

Cornbread Dressing

1 cast-iron skillet of cornbread, any recipe
1 pound Bryan's sausage
1 stick butter
1 medium onion, chopped
½ bell pepper, chopped
3 celery stalks, chopped
1 bunch green onions, chopped
8 slices toasted white bread, crumbled

4 chicken bouillon cubes, dissolved in
    2 (14.5-ounce) cans chicken broth
1 teaspoon Lawry's seasoned salt
¼ teaspoon poultry seasoning
¼ teaspoon pepper
Salt to taste
2 eggs
1 pint oysters (optional) in 1 cup boiling
    water

Make cornbread ahead of time using your favorite recipe in your iron skillet. Cook sausage until done. Add butter and all vegetables. Cook down several times, adding water and stirring. Pour mixture over crumbled cornbread and toasted bread. Add bouillon dissolved in chicken broth; mix well and add all seasonings. Add more broth, if necessary. Add raw eggs and mix well. Cover with foil and refrigerate overnight. Remove from refrigerator and add more broth if mixture is dried out. Add oysters, if desired. Bake in a 450° oven 1 hour or until the crust is brown on top. Yield: 12 generous servings.

Corn Pudding

2 (14.75-ounce) cans cream-style corn
1 stick butter, melted
1 tablespoon flour
2 tablespoons sugar

½ teaspoon salt
4 eggs, beaten
1 cup milk

Mix all ingredients together and put in a casserole dish coated with cooking spray. Bake at 350° for 50 minutes or until knife inserted comes out clean. Yield: 10 to 12 servings.

Note: May be made ahead of time and refrigerated until ready to cook.

Spinach Casserole

1 (10-ounce) package frozen spinach
1 (8-ounce) carton small-curd cottage
  cheese
3 tablespoons flour

3 eggs, lightly beaten
¼ cup butter, melted
¼ pound sharp cheese, grated

Cook spinach according to package directions and drain. Mix cottage cheese, flour, eggs, butter and grated cheese in a casserole dish. Add spinach and mix well. Bake at 350° for 1 hour. Yield: 6 servings.

Note: This can be made the night before and stored in the refrigerator. Remove from refrigerator and allow to sit 30 minutes before baking.

Sweet Potato Casserole

CASSEROLE:

1 (40-ounce) can sweet potatoes
½ cup sugar
½ cup butter

2 eggs, beaten
1 teaspoon vanilla extract
⅓ cup milk

Drain and mash sweet potatoes. Mix in sugar, butter, eggs, vanilla and milk. Place in a 1½- to 2-quart baking dish.

TOPPING:

⅓ cup butter, melted
1 cup brown sugar

½ cup flour
1 cup chopped pecans

Mix all ingredients. Sprinkle on top of sweet potato mixture. Bake at 350° for 25 minutes. Yield: 10 to 12 servings.

Note: I make this the day before, cover, and store in refrigerator overnight. I store the topping in plastic bag and crumble on top of the sweet potatoes before baking. I never liked sweet potatoes before this recipe. This is good for days after originally served, and heats in the microwave very well.

Layered Pumpkin Pie

1 (3-ounce) package cream cheese, softened
1 cup plus 1 tablespoon cold half-and-half (or milk) divided
1 tablespoon sugar
1½ cups whipped topping, thawed
1 (6-ounce) graham cracker pie crust

2 (3.4-ounce) packages vanilla instant pudding
1 (16-ounce) can pumpkin
1 teaspoon ground cinnamon
½ teaspoon ground ginger
¼ teaspoon ground cloves
Whipped topping and nuts for garnish

Mix cream cheese, 1 tablespoon half-and-half and sugar with wire whisk until smooth. Gently stir in whipped topping. Spread on bottom of crust.

Combine remaining half-and-half with pudding mix. Beat with wire whisk until well blended, 1 to 2 minutes. Let stand 3 minutes. Stir in pumpkin and spices; mix well. Spread over cream cheese layer. Refrigerate at least 2 hours. Garnish with additional whipped topping and nuts as desired. Yield: 8 servings.

Pecan-Cranberry Pie

This freezes ahead well. Take out of the freezer the night before serving.

1½ cups light corn syrup
½ cup sugar
1 cup cranberries
¼ cup butter
3 eggs, slightly beaten

1 teaspoon vanilla extract
Dash salt
1 cup pecan halves
1 (9-inch) unbaked pie shell

In a saucepan combine corn syrup, sugar, cranberries and butter. Bring to a boil. Boil gently, uncovered, 5 minutes; stir occasionally. Cool slightly.

Combine eggs, vanilla and salt. Add syrup mixture and beat well. Place pecan halves on bottom of pie shell. Pour mixture over nuts (pecans will rise to the top). Bake in 375° oven 30 to 35 minutes or until knife inserted near center comes out clean. Yield: 1 (9-inch) pie.

Lemon Curd Pound Cake

1 cup butter, softened
½ cup shortening
3 cups sugar
6 large eggs
3 cups all-purpose flour
½ teaspoon baking powder
⅛ teaspoon salt

1 cup milk
1 teaspoon vanilla extract
1 teaspoon lemon extract
Fresh rosemary sprigs, sugared
    cranberries and lemon rind strips for
    garnish

Beat butter and shortening at medium speed with an electric mixer until creamy. Gradually add sugar, beating at medium speed until light and fluffy. Add eggs, 1 at a time, beating just until the yellow yolk disappears. Sift together flour, baking powder and salt. Add flour mixture to butter mixture alternately with milk, beginning and ending with flour mixture. Beat batter at low speed just until blended after each addition. Stir in vanilla and lemon extracts. Pour batter into a greased and floured 12-cup tube pan. (Do not use a Bundt pan.) Bake at 325° for 1 hour and 30 minutes or until a long wooden pick inserted in center of cake comes out clean. Cool in pan on a wire rack 10 to 15 minutes. Remove cake from pan; carefully brush Lemon Curd over top and allow to drip down sides of cake. Cool completely on wire rack and garnish. Yield: 10 to 12 servings

LEMON CURD:

⅔ cup sugar
1½ tablespoons butter, melted
2 teaspoons grated fresh lemon rind

2 tablespoons fresh lemon juice
1 large egg, lightly beaten

Stir together first 4 ingredients in a small, heavy saucepan; add egg, stirring until blended. Cook mixture, stirring constantly, over low heat 10 to 12 minutes or until mixture thickens slightly (cooked mixture will have a thickness similar to unwhipped whipping cream) and begins to bubble around the edges. Remove from heat. The curd should be brushed immediately over cake, as mixture will continue to thicken as it cools.

Bacardi Rum Cake

This freezes ahead well. Take out of the freezer the night before serving.

1 package yellow cake mix*
1 (3.75-ounce) package vanilla pudding mix
4 eggs

½ cup cold water
½ cup Bacardi dark rum (80 Proof)
½ cup vegetable oil

Preheat oven to 325°. Grease and flour a 10-inch tube pan. Mix cake mix, pudding, eggs, water, rum and oil until smooth. Pour into prepared pan. Bake 1 hour. Cool in pan 25 minutes. Invert onto serving plate.

*If using yellow cake mix with pudding already in the mix, omit instant pudding. Use 3 eggs instead of 4, and ⅓ cup oil instead of ½ cup.

RUM GLAZE:

1 stick butter
¼ cup water

1 cup sugar
½ cup Bacardi dark rum (80 Proof)

Melt butter in saucepan. Stir in water and sugar; boil 5 minutes. Remove from heat; stir in rum. Prick top of cake all over with a toothpick. Spoon and brush Rum Glaze evenly over cake, allowing the cake to absorb the glaze.

CHOCOLATE TOPPING:

4 ounces semisweet chocolate
1 teaspoon butter or shortening

2 tablespoons chopped walnuts

Melt chocolate and butter over very low heat in heavy saucepan. When cake is cooled, drizzle Chocolate Topping over cake once Rum Glaze is absorbed. Sprinkle with nuts.

Yield: 1 (10-inch) cake.

Elegant Anniversary Dinner

Corn Bisque

Salad Greens
with Apple and Brie

Brandied Cornish Hens

Broiled Fresh Tomatoes

Wild Rice

Cherry Cheese Pie

Start your night off with an easy shrimp cocktail. Purchase a bag of frozen tail-on cooked coctail shrimp and a bottle of cocktail sauce. Fill one martini glass with shrimp and another with cocktail sauce and feed your loved one with romantic music in the background before enjoying the rest of this elegant dinner.

Corn Bisque

1 medium onion, chopped
1 clove garlic, minced
½ cup unsalted butter
¼ cup flour
2 cups claim juice
2 cups chicken broth
1 ½ cups white shoepeg corn
1 teaspoon creole seasoning
¾ fresh chopped thyme or ¼ teaspoon ground thyme
½ teaspoon cayenne pepper
½ teaspoon finely ground black pepper
2 cups half-and-half
4 green onions chopped

Sauté onion and garlic in melted butter in heavy saucepan over medium heat for 5 minutes or until translucent. Stir in flour all at once. Stir constantly for 4-5 minutes. Add clam juice and broth and bring to a boil. Stir in the corn and next 4 ingredients (seasonings). Cook uncovered over medium heat for 25 minutes, add half-and-half and continue cooking for an additional 10 minutes. Adjust seasonings to taste. Add green onions and cook 5-6 minutes. Serves 8 to 10 people

Salad Greens with Apple and Brie

**2 large Red Delicious apples, cut in thin
 wedges**
½ cup apple cider, divided
4 slices bacon

¼ cup balsamic vinegar
1 tablespoon brown sugar
6 cups mixed salad greens, torn

Dip apple wedges in ¼ cup cider to prevent browning; set aside. Cook bacon in a skillet over medium heat until crisp; remove bacon, reserving 1 tablespoon drippings in skillet. Crumble bacon and set aside.

To bacon drippings, add remaining ¼ cup cider, balsamic vinegar and brown sugar; cook dressing over medium heat, stirring constantly, until sugar dissolves. Just before serving, arrange greens, apple slices and warm Walnut Baked Brie on plates. Drizzle with dressing and sprinkle with crumbled bacon. Yield: 6 servings.

WALNUT-BAKED BRIE:

1 (8-ounce) round Brie
2 tablespoons brown sugar
¼ cup walnuts, toasted and coarsely chopped

Remove top rind from Brie. Cut cheese into 6 wedges; place on a lightly greased baking sheet. Sprinkle with brown sugar and walnuts. Bake at 450° for 2 to 3 minutes or just until soft. Serve immediately on salad greens.

Brandied Cornish Hens

2 to 4 (1¼-pound) Cornish hens
⅓ cup chopped fresh parsley
½ teaspoon salt
½ cup butter, softened and divided
½ cup red currant jelly
½ cup brandy

Remove giblets from hens; reserve for another use. Rinse hens with cold water and pat dry. Combine parsley, salt and ¼ cup butter; mix well. Stuff cavity of hens with parsley mixture and truss securely. Place hens breast side up in a shallow baking pan. Rub hens with remaining ¼ cup butter. Bake at 375° for 30 minutes.

Combine jelly and brandy in a small saucepan; cook over low heat, stirring often, until jelly melts. Spoon half of jelly mixture over hens and bake 30 additional minutes; baste every 5 to 10 minutes with remaining jelly mixture and pan drippings. Yield: 2 to 4 servings. Birds can be halved for light eaters.

Broiled Fresh Tomatoes

4 fresh tomatoes
2 tablespoons melted butter
Salt and pepper to taste
¼ cup grated Parmesan cheese

Cut tomatoes in thick slices and place in a greased shallow baking dish. Brush with butter and sprinkle with salt and pepper. Sprinkle with cheese. Broil about 6 inches from heat 15 minutes or until cheese is lightly browned.

Cherry Cheese Pie

1 (8-ounce) package cream cheese, softened
1 (14-ounce) can sweetened condensed milk
½ cup reconstituted lemon juice
1 teaspoon vanilla extract
1 (9-inch) graham cracker crumb crust

Cherry pie filling, chilled

In medium bowl, beat cream cheese until light and fluffy. Add sweetened condensed milk; blend thoroughly. Stir in lemon juice and vanilla. Pour into crust. Chill 2 hours or until set. Top with desired amount of pie filling before serving. Refrigerate any leftovers.

Note: Any of your favorite fruit pie fillings or toppings can be substituted for cherry pie filling.

Saturday Night Supper

Black Bean Dip

Chilled Corn Salad

Rotel Chicken and Spaghetti

Serve With:

Green Peas

Dinner Rolls

Mom's Apple Pie in a Jar (page 58)

Carrot Cake Jam (page 56)

Coca-Cola Cake

This is a quick Saturday night supper that can be eaten early so you and your friends can catch a good movie. Invite your guests to arrive at 5:00 p.m. and end by 6:30 p.m. in time to catch that movie, play or concert you want to see! I'm sharing Mom's Apple Pie in a Jar and Carrot Cake Jam recipes as condiments to spread on the dinner rolls. This is a great addition to this meal.

Black Bean Dip

1 (15-ounce) can black beans, drained
1 (8-ounce) can tomato sauce
1 cup shredded Cheddar or Mexican cheese, divided
1 teaspoon chili powder
Chopped fresh cilantro for garnish

Combine beans and tomato sauce in a saucepan; bring to a boil over medium heat, stirring occasionally. Remove from heat. Mash beans with a potato masher or the back of a spoon. Add ½ cup cheese and chili powder; cook, stirring constantly, until cheese melts. Pour into a serving bowl and garnish with remaining ½ cup shredded cheese and chopped cilantro. Serve dip warm with tortilla chips or pita chips. Yield: 2 cups.

Chilled Corn Salad

1 (12-ounce) can whole-kernel corn, drained
1 small onion, chopped
½ cup chopped green onion
2 tablespoons minced fresh parsley
2 tablespoons cider vinegar
1 tablespoon vegetable oil
¼ teaspoon salt
¼ teaspoon black pepper

Combine all ingredients. Cover and chill at least 4 hours before serving. Yield: 4 servings.

Note: This salad is beautiful served atop fresh tomato slices. This makes a very colorful side dish.

Rotel Chicken and Spaghetti

1 pound Velveeta cheese
1 (10-ounce) can diced Rotel tomatoes
    and green chiles
1 pound spaghetti, cooked

1 cooked chicken, skinned, boned
    and cut in pieces (or substitute with
    1 [12.5-ounce] can cooked chicken
    breast)

Melt cheese in microwave, add Rotel tomatoes and stir. Combine spaghetti and chicken. Add cheese mixture and mix well. Place in a 9x13-inch greased pan and bake at 350° for 30 minutes.

Coca-Cola Cake

2 cups sugar
2 cups flour
1 cup Coca-Cola
½ cup butter
½ cup Crisco oil
3 tablespoons cocoa

2 eggs, beaten
½ cup buttermilk
1 teaspoon baking soda
1 teaspoon vanilla extract
1½ cups miniature marshmallows

Sift together sugar and flour; set aside. Bring Coca-Cola, butter, oil, and cocoa to a boil; remove from heat, and add to the sugar and flour mixture. Add eggs and mix. Add buttermilk, baking soda, vanilla and marshmallows. Mix well and bake in a greased and floured 9x13-inch pan at 350° for 40 minutes or until done.

FROSTING:

½ cup butter
⅓ cup Coca-Cola
3 tablespoons cocoa

1 (1-pound) box powdered sugar
1 cup chopped nuts
1 cup miniature marshmallows

Bring butter, Coca-Cola and cocoa to a boil. Remove from heat and add powdered sugar, nuts and marshmallows. Mix well and spread over top of cake as soon as cake is removed from the oven and is still in the pan. Let cake cool before serving. Yield: 20 servings.

Sunday Night Supper

Easy Appetizer:
Assorted Veggies and Dip

Black-Eyed Pea Salad

Cream Cheese Potatoes

Italian Pot Roast

Broccoli Mold with Mushrooms

Soda Pop Cake

Invite your friends over to enjoy your favorite team play footfall Sunday afternoon, and hopefully you won't suffer from heartburn before supper! Everything can be prepared the day before except the roast. If you're a football fanatic like me, you can enjoy the game, too. In our house, it's the Dallas Cowboys!

The Black-Eyed Pea Salad and Italian Pot Roast sound "down home"; but make no mistake, the Cream Cheese Potatoes and Broccoli Mold with Mushrooms are showy side dishes.

Black-Eyed Pea Salad

2 (1-pound) cans black-eyed peas, drained
1 onion, sliced thin
½ cup olive oil
¼ cup wine vinegar
2 garlic cloves, mashed
1 tablespoon Worcestershire sauce

1 teaspoon salt
Pepper to taste
1 bay leaf
8 lettuce leaves
Salsa for garnish

Put peas and onion in a heat-resistant bowl. In a saucepan, combine oil, wine vinegar, garlic, Worcestershire, salt, pepper and bay leaf. Bring to a boil and pour over peas and onion. Cover and refrigerate several hours before serving. Serve over lettuce leaves and garnish with salsa. The salsa makes the salad very colorful and adds zip. Yield: 8 servings.

Cream Cheese Potatoes

10 medium potatoes, cooked
Milk
1 (8-ounce) package cream cheese,
   softened

1 cup sour cream
1 teaspoon garlic salt
Butter
Paprika

Beat cooked potatoes with electric mixer until smooth, adding enough milk to moisten. Add cream cheese, sour cream and garlic salt; beat until mixed. Place in a 2-quart casserole dish and dot with butter. Sprinkle with paprika. Bake at 350° for 30 minutes. Yield: 12 servings.

Italian Pot Roast

1 (2- to 3-pound) boneless beef chuck roast
1 teaspoon salt
½ teaspoon freshly ground pepper
4 tablespoons all-purpose flour, divided
2 tablespoons vegetable oil
½ cup water, divided
¼ cup ketchup
½ teaspoon dried marjoram
½ teaspoon dried rosemary
½ teaspoon dried thyme
1 teaspoon Italian seasoning
¼ teaspoon dry mustard
2 garlic cloves, minced
½ cup dry sherry
1 bay leaf
1 tablespoon minced onion

Sprinkle roast with salt, pepper and 2 tablespoons flour. Heat oil in a large Dutch oven and brown all sides of roast. Combine ¼ cup water and remaining ingredients except the 2 tablespoons flour; pour over roast. Bring to a boil over medium heat; cover, reduce heat and simmer 1½ hours or until roast is tender.

Remove roast, reserving liquid in Dutch oven. Remove and discard bay leaf. Combine remaining ¼ cup water and remaining 2 tablespoons flour, stirring until smooth. Add flour mixture to liquid in Dutch oven, stirring constantly, and bring to a boil over medium heat. Boil, stirring constantly, until gravy thickens. Serve gravy with roast. Yield: 6 servings.

Broccoli Mold with Mushrooms

A beautiful ring filled with sautéed mushrooms for a buffet.

2 (10-ounce) packages frozen chopped broccoli
3 tablespoons butter
3 tablespoons flour
¼ cup chicken broth
1 cup sour cream
⅓ cup minced green onions, tops included
3 eggs, beaten
¾ cup grated Swiss cheese
½ cup slivered almonds, toasted
1 teaspoon salt
½ teaspoon pepper
½ to 1 teaspoon nutmeg

Cook broccoli in 1 cup salted water until barely tender; drain thoroughly and chop fine. (Don't use your blender—or you'll have baby food.) Heat butter in a skillet and whisk in flour until smooth. Gradually add chicken broth and sour cream. Add green onion and cook over low heat, stirring until thick and blended. Stir beaten eggs into sauce and cook 1 minute, stirring constantly; blend in cheese until melted. Add broccoli, almonds and seasonings, adding more salt and pepper if desired. Spoon mixture into an oiled 1-quart ring mold. Bake at 350° in a hot water bath 50 minutes or until a knife inserted in center is clean. Marvelous to do ahead and freeze. May be placed in the oven frozen, but increase baking time about 30 minutes. Yield: 8 servings.

Note: May also pour into 8 (5-ounce) custard cups, and bake 30 minutes.

Soda Pop Cake

1 yellow cake mix plus ingredients to make

2 (3-ounce) packages strawberry gelatin

1½ cups boiling water

1 (12-ounce) can cream soda

1 (3.4-ounce) box vanilla instant pudding mix

1½ cups milk

1 (8-ounce) carton whipped topping

Bake yellow cake in a 9x13-inch cake pan according to package directions. Prick top of cake with a toothpick. Mix strawberry gelatin with boiling water until dissolved. Add cream soda to gelatin mixture and slowly pour over baked cake. Cool cake thoroughly. Mix pudding with milk. Fold in whipped topping until mixed and then pour over cake and spread to cover. Refrigerate until ready to serve. Yield: 12 servings.

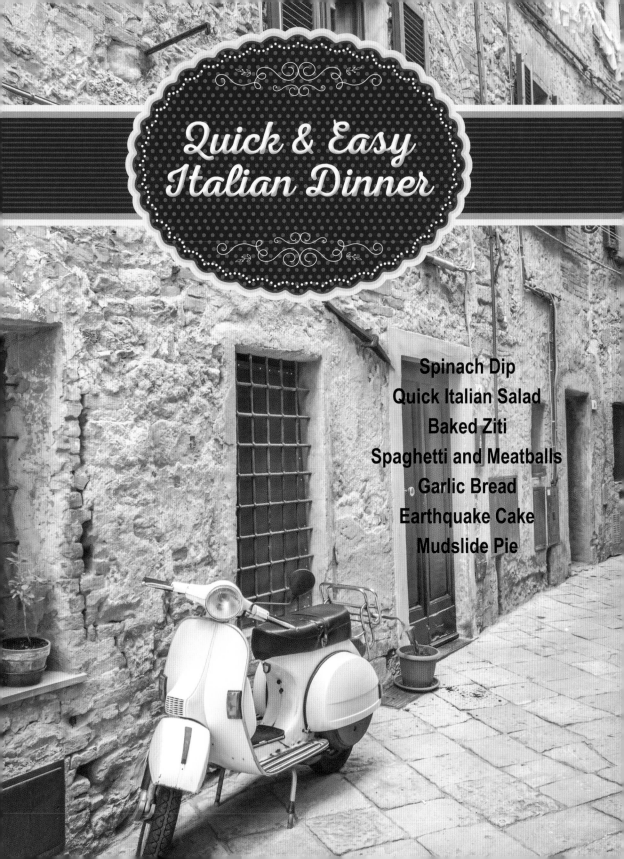

Quick & Easy Italian Dinner

Spinach Dip
Quick Italian Salad
Baked Ziti
Spaghetti and Meatballs
Garlic Bread
Earthquake Cake
Mudslide Pie

Spinach Dip

1 (10.5-ounce) package frozen chopped
    spinach
1 (0.4-ounce) package Knorr vegetable
    soup mix

1½ cups sour cream
1 cup real mayonnaise
1 (8-ounce) can water chestnuts, chopped
3 green onions, chopped

Thaw spinach and squeeze dry. Stir soup mix, sour cream and mayonnaise until well blended. Stir in spinach, water chestnuts and green onions. Cover and chill 2 hours. Stir before serving. Yield: 4 cups.

Quick Italian Salad

1 (10-ounce) bag pre-washed Italian salad
    greens
Grape tomatoes, halved

Feta cheese, crumbled
Fresh basil, chopped
Balsamic or Italian dressing of choice

Place salad greens in a large salad bowl. Top with tomatoes, feta cheese and fresh basil to taste. Toss gently with dressing before serving. Yield: 6 servings.

Baked Ziti

1 pound ground sausage
1 (10-ounce) box rigatoni pasta
1 (26-ounce) jar spaghetti sauce
5-6 slices smoked provolone cheese

1 pint sour cream
1 cup grated Parmesan cheese
1 (8-ounce) package shredded mozzarella
    cheese

Brown sausage in a large skillet. Cook pasta according to package directions; drain. In a large casserole, layer half the pasta; top with half the spaghetti sauce. Place provolone cheese slices on top; cover with sour cream and then cooked sausage. Add another layer of pasta and remaining sauce. Top with Parmesan and mozzarella cheeses. Bake at 350° for 30 to 40 minutes until slightly browned. Yield: 10 to 12 servings.

Spaghetti and Meatballs

MEATBALLS:

2 eggs
½ cup milk
3 slices white bread, torn
2 pounds ground chuck
½ cup finely chopped onion

2 tablespoons chopped parsley
1 garlic clove, crushed
1 teaspoon salt
½ teaspoon pepper

Preheat oven to 450°. In medium bowl, beat eggs slightly. Add milk and torn bread; mix well. Let stand 5 minutes. Add ground chuck, onion, parsley, garlic, salt and pepper; mix until well blended. Shape into 24 meatballs, 1½ inches in diameter. Place in a well-greased shallow baking pan. Bake uncovered, 30 minutes.

SAUCE:

¼ cup olive oil (or salad oil)
½ cup chopped onion
2 garlic cloves, crushed
2 tablespoons sugar
1 tablespoon salt
1½ teaspoons dried basil
½ teaspoon fennel seed

¼ teaspoon pepper
1 (2-pound, 3-ounce) can Italian-style tomatoes
2 (6-ounce) cans tomato paste
½ cup water
1 (1-pound) package spaghetti
½ cup grated Parmesan cheese

Heat oil in a 5-quart Dutch oven over medium heat; sauté onion and garlic until golden. Add remaining Sauce ingredients, except spaghetti and Parmesan, mashing tomatoes with wooden spoon. Bring to a boil. Reduce heat and simmer, covered, 30 minutes. Add Meatballs and drippings; simmer, covered, 1 hour, stirring occasionally. Cook spaghetti according to package directions; drain.

To serve: Place spaghetti on serving dish. Top with Meatballs and Sauce. Sprinkle with Parmesan. Yield: 6 servings. The Sauce recipe can be doubled for 12 servings.

Note: Frozen Italian meatballs may be substituted. They are very good and cut down on the preparation time. Just make the sauce and add frozen meatballs.

Garlic Bread

Prepared garlic spread   **1 loaf French bread, sliced**

Spread garlic spread on bread. Wrap in foil and heat at 350° until warm (approximately 20 minutes).

Earthquake Cake

The main caution for anyone who wants to make an Earthquake Cake is not to try to squeeze it into a smaller pan than specified. You want an earthquake, not a volcano. This rich chocolate cake is ideal for shipping, because nothing more can happen to its looks, and it's so delicious—it's always welcome.

½ cup chopped nuts
1¼ cups sweetened flaked coconut
1 box German chocolate cake mix, batter prepared according to package directions
½ cup butter
1 (8-ounce) package cream cheese, softened
1 (1-pound) box powdered sugar

Heat oven to 350°. Grease a 9x13-inch cake pan. Cover bottom of the pan with nuts and coconut. Pour prepared cake batter on top. Melt butter in a bowl in microwave. Add cream cheese and powdered sugar; stir to blend. Spoon over unbaked batter. Bake 40 minutes. Yield: 18 servings.

The icing sinks into the batter as it bakes, forming the white ribbon inside.

Note: You cannot test for doneness with a cake test, as the cake will appear sticky even when it is done.

Mudslide Pie

The earthquake is not a pretty dessert. It is very good; but if you prefer, here is a luscious pie that everyone will love! So simple, yet so delicious!

CRUST:

1½ cups chocolate graham cracker crumbs
6 tablespoons butter, melted

Mix crumbs and butter and pour into a 9- or 10-inch pie plate. Press crumbs over the bottom and the sides and refrigerate until firm.

FILLING:

Simple Vanilla Ice Cream made with a Cuisinart frozen yogurt/ice cream maker.

2 cups heavy cream, chilled
1 (200-ml) bottle Kahlúa Mudslide (approximately 1 cup)
¾ cup sugar
1 teaspoon vanilla extract

Combine all ice cream ingredients and stir well. Pour into machine, turn on, and in 20 to 25 minutes pour ice cream into the chilled pie crust.

OPTION WITH STORE-BOUGHT VANILLA ICE CREAM:

1 quart (or 2 pints) vanilla ice cream, softened
1 (200-ml) bottle Kahlúa Mudslide (approximately 1 cup)

Fill a blender three-quarters full with ice cream, add Mudslide and mix. Pour into crust, as above.

TOPPING:

Frozen whipped topping   **Mini chocolate chips for garnish**

Top with frozen whipped topping and garnish with mini chocolate chips. Keep pie frozen until time to serve. Yield: 6 to 8 servings

Note: Non-drinkers should not be bothered by the small amount of alcohol in the Kahlúa Mudslide.

Last-Minute Dinner Guest

WELCOME

Easy Appetizer:
Cheddar Cheese and Pepper Jack Cheese with Assorted Crackers

Wild Rice Salad

Easy Pork Chops

Buttered Noodles

Danish Tomatoes

Dump Cake

Basic Vanilla Cream Pie with Variations (p 236)

This whole meal can be put together in 30 minutes and ready to eat in an hour. High school or college friends passing through will be impressed with how quickly you put this on the table. It's good, too!

Wild Rice Salad

1 (13.75-ounce) can beef or chicken broth, divided
1 (6-ounce) package long-grain and wild rice
1 (11-ounce) can mandarin oranges, drained
1 (8-ounce) can sliced water chestnuts, drained
¼ cup sliced scallions
⅓ cup mayonnaise

Reserve 2 tablespoons broth, and add enough water to remaining broth to substitute for water in rice package directions.

Cook rice according to directions, omitting butter, and substituting broth for water; cool. Stir in oranges, water chestnuts and scallions. Blend reserved 2 tablespoons broth and mayonnaise; stir into rice mixture. Cover and refrigerate 2 to 3 hours. Serve on lettuce leaves. Yield: 6 to 8 servings.

Note: For quick cooling, put in the quick-freeze portion of your freezer; stir often. Fix this before beginning the rest of the meal.

Easy Pork Chops

4 pork chops, any cut
Salt and pepper to taste
½ stick butter
1 (10.75-ounce) can cream of mushroom soup
1 soup can water

Season pork chops with salt and pepper. Melt butter in skillet. Brown pork chops on both sides. Remove chops and add soup to skillet. Add water and stir over low heat till smooth. Return chops to skillet; reduce heat to simmer. Cover and cook until done. Serve with Buttered Noodles (recipe on next page). Yield: 4 servings.

Buttered Noodles

1 (8-ounce) package noodles
½ stick butter

Parsley flakes to taste

Prepare noodles according to package directions; drain. Add butter; stir until melted. Add parsley flakes. Yield: 4 to 6 servings.

Danish Tomatoes

Fresh tomatoes
Sugar to taste
Salt to taste

Buttered croutons
Crumbled blue cheese

Cut tops off tomatoes and cut almost through into wedges. Spread to resemble flowers. Sprinkle with sugar and salt and place in a shallow pan. Bake at 375° for 10 minutes. Add the croutons and blue cheese. Bake until the cheese bubbles.

Dump Cake

1 (1-pound, 6-ounce) can cherry pie filling
1 (8.25-ounce) can crushed pineapple, undrained

1 (18.25-ounce) box yellow cake mix
2 sticks butter, melted
1 (3.5-ounce) can flake coconut
2 cups chopped pecans

In a 9x13-inch pan, layer all ingredients in order listed above. Bake in a 350° oven 45 minutes. Yield: 12 servings.

Cream Pies

Here is one of the best basic recipes I have found and it has so many variations. I will share a few of them with you. The sky is the limit on all the different pies you can make. It is very easy and depending on the pie shell and topping you choose, it can be put together in 20 minutes or less not counting the cooling time for the filling.

CRUST:

Choose your pie shell. It can be the traditional pastry pie shell, homemade or frozen. Or a crumb crust: graham cracker, vanilla wafer, chocolate graham cracker or chocolate wafer. You can choose any cookie you have on hand and make a crumb crust.

TOPPING:

Choose your topping. Whipped cream, frozen topping, whipped topping in aerosol can, canned pie filling, fresh fruit or meringue.

Basic Vanilla Cream Pie

FILLING:

1 cup sugar
⅓ cup cornstarch
¼ teaspoon salt
3 cups milk

4 egg yolks, beaten
4 tablespoons butter
1 teaspoon vanilla extract

Mix sugar, cornstarch and salt together in a large microwave-safe glass bowl. Whisk in milk and beaten egg yolks.

Microwave on high power 5 minutes; remove and stir. Continue cooking at 2-minute intervals, stirring after each. Repeat 2 to 3 times until the total cook time is between 10 and 12 minutes. Mixture should be thick.

Stir in butter and vanilla. Pour into pie shell of choice. Cool and add topping of choice.

VARIATIONS:

Add additional ingredients once the filling is cooked. These are just a few variations—see how many different variations you can dream up in your kitchen! Have fun.

Coconut Pie

Substitute coconut flavoring for vanilla and stir in 1 cup coconut.

Chocolate Pie

Stir in 1 cup chocolate chips, 2 ounces baking chocolate, or ½ cup cocoa.

Lemon Pie

Substitute lemon flavoring for vanilla; add ⅓ cup lemon juice and 1 teaspoon grated lemon peel (optional).

Mounds Pie

Add coconut flavoring, 1 cup chocolate chips and 1 cup coconut

Butterscotch Pie

Stir in 1cup butterscotch chips.

Peanut Butter Pie

Stir in 1 cup peanut butter chips or 1 cup Reese's mini peanut butter cups.

Quick & Easy Appetizers

Any of the following can be served in your favorite serving dish and garnished appropriately with lemon or lime slices, rose radish, pansies, strawberry, mint sprig, rosemary sprig, basil, parsley or cilantro.

- Can of bean dip, heated with shredded cheese on top. Serve with tortilla chips.

- Onion dip is so easy to do, and I prefer this to store-bought. Stir together ½ pint sour cream and one envelope onion soup mix; chill and serve with your favorite chips.

- Any of the soft, flavored cream cheeses. Serve garden dill with your favorite crackers and fruit flavored with gingersnaps, vanilla wafers or crackers.

- Always keep a block of cream cheese on hand. The appetizers you can quickly make with a block of cream cheese are endless.

Shrimp Cocktail Spread

1 (8-ounce) jar shrimp cocktail
1 (8-ounce) block cream cheese, softened

Pour shrimp cocktail over block of cream cheese. Garnish with lemon and serve with crackers.

Spicy Spread

1 (10-ounce) bottle Heinz 57 sauce
1 (8-ounce) block cream cheese

Pour Heinz 57 over block of cream cheese. Garnish with parsley or fresh basil; serve with crackers.

Salsa Spread

1 (16-ounce) jar your favorite salsa
1 (8-ounce) block cream cheese

Pour salsa over block of cream cheese. Garnish with fresh cilantro and serve with crackers.

Pepper Spread

1 (8-ounce) jar hot pepper jelly
1 (8-ounce) block cream cheese

Pour hot pepper jelly over block of cream cheese. Serve with crackers.

You get the picture—try your own creations; all you need is 1 (8-ounce) block of softened cream cheese, softened. Pour anything you like over the block. Use chutney, any fruit salsa, preserves or whole cranberry sauce. Always have a variety of garnishes and crackers available.

Party Meatballs, Little Smokies, Chicken Chunks, Franks or Sausage

1 (8-ounce) jar grape jelly
1 (12-ounce) bottle chili sauce

In a slow cooker, melt jelly and add chili sauce. Add any of the above ingredients, and you'll have a great appetizer. Serve in a chafing dish for special occasions.

Vegetable Tray

1 bag mixed broccoli, cauliflower and carrots found in bagged salad area
1 bottle or jar of your favorite salad dressing or dip

Arrange vegetables on a serving tray around a bowl of dip.

Pickled Tray

Raid your pantry and refrigerator:

Pickles, dill or sweet
Pickled okra and/or corn
Olives, green and/or black
Marinated artichoke hearts

Arrange on a serving tray with a block of cheese. Serve with crackers.

Rotel Cheese Dip

1 (10-ounce) can Rotel diced tomatoes and green chiles
1 (15-ounce) can chili without beans, optional
1 (15-ounce) can black beans, drained and rinsed, optional
1 pound Velveeta cheese, melted

Add Rotel tomatoes, chili and beans to melted cheese. Serve warm in a small slow cooker with assorted tortilla chips.

Putting a Meal Together

Appetizers

Salad or Soup

Entrée

Potato, Rice or Noodles

Vegetables

Dessert

Take advantage of all the boxed, canned, and frozen items in the grocery store to cut down on prep time and still have a meal you can be proud to serve your family and guests. Quick and simple meals can be very appealing and enjoyable. If I have a well-stocked pantry and freezer, I can just put my mind on autopilot and within 30 minutes, I have a complete meal.

Appetizers

For family meals, I do not use appetizers, especially if the guests have children. Children get full easier and more quickly than adults. You want them to eat the other menu items which are more important to their growth. For parties, I usually keep appetizers as simple and small as possible so my guests have an appetite for the meal I've prepared.

Salad or Soup

Choose bagged pre-washed salad greens. Add tomato, cucumber, yellow squash, zucchini, avocado, drained mandarin oranges, almonds, pecans, walnuts, sunflower seeds, dried cranberries, cheese (crumbled Blue cheese, feta cheese, grated Cheddar or Jack, etc.)—basically anything you like. Add your favorite dressing, and there's your salad.

Entrée

Choose a cut of meat—steak, fish or chicken breasts. Season with your favorite seasoning: McCormick steak seasoning for steak, lemon pepper for fish, celery salt or Greek seasoning for chicken. Broil, rotisserie or grill meat.

Potato, Rice or Noodles

Instant potatoes are not what they once were. Betty Crocker's are great, and there are several flavors to choose from: Three-cheese, Roasted Garlic and Herb, Butter and Herb, to name a few. There are also many rice and noodle dishes offered in pouches. Lipton does a good job, and store brands offer a good, tasty selection as well. Baked potatoes are always good. A medium potato can be microwaved in 5 minutes.

Vegetables

As a young adult, I was introduced to a wide variety of fresh vegetables, and I developed a taste for many different things:

Purple-hull peas	Fried green tomatoes
Crowder peas	Squash pickles
Cream peas	Okra (boiled and fried)
Speckled butter beans	Pinto beans
Lima beans	Eggplant
Yellow squash	Spinach
Zucchini	Greens of all sort

Fresh vegetables are always the best. Here are some of my favorites:

Green beans	Cabbage
Home grown tomatoes	Carrots
Red potatoes	Corn on cob, creamed, whole kernel
English peas	

- Frozen veggies can be easily prepared in the pressure cooker. Season with a little salt and pepper. Add 1 tablespoon of rendered bacon grease or a slice of crisply cooked bacon for flavor in the pressure cooker (rack removed) and cook 3 minutes. Irresistible!

- Most people I talk to are afraid to use pressure cookers—but only because they have no experience with them. They are a cooking wonder, and I use them for frozen vegetables as well as fresh. This method is really like steaming.

- Canned veggies, peas, and beans can be cooked on the stove top with bacon or rendered bacon fat. Just bring to a boil and reduce liquid by half.

- Today, most of us have access to fresh home grown vegetables at our local farmers market. Cook fresh vegetables in the pressure cooker as you would cook frozen.

Buy fresh vegetables in large quantities when in season, and freeze to enjoy all winter. Most are very easy to prepare for the freezer. Blanch fresh vegetables in boiling water 3 minutes, drain, cool, and store in freezer bags. The taste difference is negligible.

Fresh green beans are easy to prepare for the freezer. Just trim off the ends. (I use kitchen shears.) Cut green beans in equal lengths. Place in boiling water 3 minutes; drain and cool. I place mine in ice water to stop the cooking process. They are cool and ready for the freezer bags in 10 minutes. To cook, remove amount needed, place in a pressure cooker (rack removed). Add 1 tablespoon rendered bacon grease and cook 3 minutes. You can also add small, well-washed new potatoes to the green beans. They are great.

Buy all fresh peas and beans (except green beans) shelled. Do not wash after shelling; just place in freezer bags and freeze.

• For fried okra, squash, zucchini, eggplant, and green tomatoes, wash, trim off ends, slice, dip in an egg wash, and dredge in cornmeal mix. Place on a plate and refrigerate 30 to 45 minutes to dry. Then place in plastic freezer bags for storage. To cook, remove amount needed. Heat cooking oil to 400° and fry until golden. A deep-fat fryer is the best to use here. (You don't have to stir constantly or turn veggies over.) You can serve as is or serve with a cheese sauce. My favorite is the Rotel Cheese Dip (page 146).

• Squash, zucchini, cabbage, spinach and other greens, corn on the cob, and carrots are always available fresh in your grocery, so I wouldn't take the time or use my valuable freezer space for these veggies.

• Dried beans and peas are always good, but preparation time is lengthy. However, after the soaking, they can be cooked in a slow cooker 8 to 10 hours and be ready for dinner. Prior planning is obviously needed here. I use ham hocks, hog jowl, bacon, meaty ham bone, or Polish or kielbasa sausage to flavor the beans along with a stalk of celery, a little onion, salt, and pepper. These actually can be a whole meal in themselves with cornbread and a salad or slaw.

Whatever vegetable you choose, in whatever form you
choose, it is an absolute must to complete a meal.

Desserts

This is my favorite part of the meal, and I do enjoy baking. But for those who don't, there are so many things already prepared that can be used, from frozen cakes and pies that only need defrosting, to boxed cheesecakes which take minimal time to prepare, cake mixes and canned frostings, cookies, fresh fruits in season, ice cream, frozen yogurt. You can always pick up pastries in your local bakery.

Now, you can choose your favorites and put together a
menu to please everyone's palate. Bon Appétit!

Index

**The Ultimate Venison
Cookbook for Deer Camp**
$21.95 • 288 pages • 7x10
paperbound • full color

Game for all Seasons Cookbook
$16.95 • 240 pages • 7x10
paperbound • full color

Church Recipes are the Best

Georgia Church Suppers
$18.95 • 256 pages • 7x10 • paperbound • full color

Mississippi Church Suppers
$21.95 • 288 pages • 7x10 • paperbound • full color

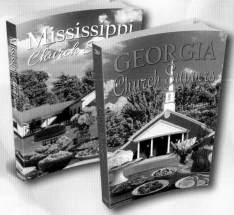

It's So Easy...
to Cook Food Your Family Will Love...

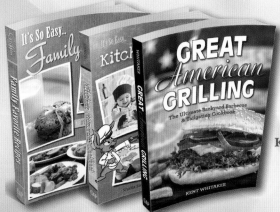

Great American Grilling
$21.95 • 288 pages • 7x10
paperbound • full color

Kitchen Memories • Family Favorite Recipes
EACH: $18.95 • 256 pages • 7x10
paperbound • full color

Eat & Explore State Cookbook Series

This series is a favorite of local cooks, armchair travelers, and cookbook collectors across the nation.
EACH: **$18.95 • 256 pages • 7x9 • paperbound**

Arkansas • Illinois • Minnesota • North Carolina
Ohio • Oklahoma • Virginia • Washington

State Hometown Cookbook Series

A Hometown Taste of America, One State at a Time

Each state's charm is revealed through local recipes from resident cooks along with stories and photos that will take you back to your hometown ...or take you on a journey to explore other hometowns across the country.
EACH: **$18.95 • 256 pages • 8x9 • paperbound • full color**

Alabama • Georgia • Louisiana • Mississippi
South Carolina • Tennessee • Texas • West Virginia

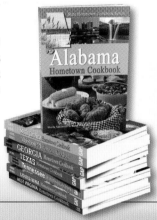

State Back Road Restaurants Series

Every Road Leads to Delicious Food

From two-lane highways and interstates, to dirt roads and quaint downtowns, every road leads to delicious food when traveling across our United States. Each well-researched and charming guide leads you to the state's best back road restaurants. No time to travel? No problem. Each restaurant shares their favorite recipes—their signature dish, or a family favorite, always delicious.
EACH: **$18.95 • 256 pages • 7x9 • paperbound • full color**

Alabama • Kentucky • Louisiana • Missouri • Tennessee • Texas

Betty B's Having a Party!
A Holiday Dinner Party Cookbook
Betty B's having a party.. and now you can too.. with 32 menus for holiday-themed parties that will make your friends and family rave.
$18.95 • 256 pages • 7x9 • paperbound • full color

Little Gulf Coast Seafood Cookbook
$14.95 • 192 pages • 5½x8½
paperbound • full color

3 Easy Ways to Order

1) Call toll-free **1-888-854-5954** to order by phone or to request a free catalog.

2) Order online at **www.GreatAmericanPublishers.com**

3) Mail a check or money order for the cost of the book(s) plus $4 shipping for the first book and $1 each additional (6 or more = free shipping) plus a list of the books you want to order along with your name, address, phone and email to:

Great American Publishers
501 Avalon Way Suite B
Brandon MS 39047

Find us on facebook: www.facebook.com/GreatAmericanPublishers

Join the We Love 2 Cook Club and get a 20% discount.

www.GreatAmericanPublishers.com